C000225304

The Secret ___, __
of Mothers

Edited by

Maggie Gordon-Walker

and

Charlotte Naughton

SILVERDART PUBLISHING
MMXVIII

Mothers Uncovered
www.mothersuncovered.com
+44 (0) 1273 235336
maggie@mothersuncovered.com

Silverdart Publishing
Woodmancote Manor, Cirencester
Gloucestershire GL7 7ED
www.silverdart.co.uk
+44 (0) 1285 831789
info@silverdart.co.uk

ISBN-13   978-0-9554581-9-4

Cover photo credits:
Front cover and back cover group - Cécile Chevalier.
Other back cover photos - Kerry Ghais.

For Robin, Luke and Rowan

Contents

Foreword

Caroline Lucas
MP for Brighton Pavilion

I became aware of Mothers Uncovered, and their founder, the brilliant, dynamic and formidable Maggie Gordon-Walker, back in 2010, just a few years after it was formed. Since then, I've had the opportunity to see the amazing work that Mothers Uncovered do to help women navigate the early days of motherhood and beyond.

As a mum of two (now adult) boys, I still clearly remember the overwhelming responsibility I felt being left in charge of such incredibly precious new people for the first time. I was sometimes so stressed that I had a recurring nightmare of leaving my briefcase with the childminder and bringing my child to work. There is no rule book. Alongside the overwhelming feelings of love, excitement, and hope, there was also lots of fear, worry and utter, bone-wrenching exhaustion. It was the start of a brilliant rollercoaster, just one that you can't actually get off – so it's a case of finding ways to ride out the down moments and finding the times and spaces to celebrate the good.

Life as a new mother can feel all-consuming, so groups like Mothers Uncovered are hugely important - they recognise that post-natal support to tackle such a momentous life change is every bit as important as pre-natal support which focuses on the physical aspect of

Caroline Lucas, left, with Maggie Gordon-Walker
Photo: Gideon Fisher

childbirth. Mothers Uncovered offers a safe and supportive space, with reassurance that there's no 'right' way to feel – and that the times of feeling sadness, frustration and even anger don't make us 'bad' parents. In childbirth, we lose something of who we were as well as gaining something new and infinitely precious – and the changes can be disorientating.

In this volume, you'll find poetry and prose, ecstasy and despair, searing honesty and wicked humour. It's a testament to creativity, courage and love – and above all, joyous and defiant hope.

How this book came into being

Since 2008, Mothers Uncovered has run 30 groups across Brighton, Hove and Lewes in children's centres, community centres, youth centres and the Women's Centre.

We created a show for the 2009 Brighton Fringe based on interviews with four mothers.

We ran a writing group that produced a show featuring in the Adult Learning Festival in 2010.

Some mothers recorded their stories for the Mass Observation project based at the University of Sussex in 2010.

We ran three large-scale, all-day events called Big Sunday and Mother Nurture in 2012, 2013 and 2014.

We have created improvised shows that have run in fringe venues.

Mothers Uncovered was a community partner for the University of Brighton's New Practices Seminar Series (2016) and the lead partner on a Peer Support Project (2014).

Photographs from the sessions have featured in the Brighton Photo Fringe and been displayed at various centres.

All along, women have had their voices heard, through their writing and through interviews. I have wanted to compile a book of their experiences for some years, but have never had the funding. This year, to mark our 10th anniversary, I thought we should just do it anyway.

For this book, 'Your Stories' refers to the writing group that took place in 2010 for the Adult Learning Festival. Other articles and experiences have been submitted at various points, some of which appear on the Mothers Uncovered blog.

The interviews were conducted by Lesley Hughes and myself in 2009, 2010 and 2011. While all the women were happy for their interviews to be used, some requested to be anonymous. There is something more unguarded about an interview transcript. For this reason, we have ascribed a letter in place of a name for each interviewee, and have removed identifying names and details. There were 22 women in total whose interviews appear in the book. The age of their child at the time of the interview is given. I always found it comforting to know the age of the baby when I was hearing about a woman's experience.

My thanks go to my fabulous facilitator, transcriber and co-editor Charlotte Naughton, and Sarah Warbrick, who also helped transcribe.

Thanks also to Alex Murray, along with John and Jennifer, at Silverdart; to my facilitators over the years; and, of course, to all the mothers who have shared their stories.

Maggie Gordon-Walker

List of contributors

This book is a collective effort, with over 50 women's stories and experiences. The contributors include:

Maggie Gordon-Walker –
maggiegordon-walker.com
Morgan Nichols –
tinyurl.com/gwsr4wx
Chiara Corrao –
dilloconparoletue.wordpress.com
Charlotte Naughton
Claire Robinson –
allgristtothemill.wordpress.com
Ali Norrell
Lesley Hughes
Rebecca Tonge
Claire Jones-Hughes
Chloe Forfitt
Julie Canavan
Megan Kendall
Ellen Stewart
Saskia Neary
Anna Kisby
Caren Fisher

Rebecca Santos
Kate Ballard
Jenny Birchall
Sam Johnson
Ione Milner-Gulland
Hanora Power-Dow
Gemma Painter
Melinda Clark
Heidi Brydon
Felicity Beckett
Jo Aldred
Lou Noble
Charlotte Hartley-Jones
Mia Taylor
Jessica Cabrillana Cruz
Sally Amor
Nicky Walter
Clare Graham
Khadine Morcom
Ilona Gadjics

In addition, 17 other mothers, who prefer to remain anonymous, provided written material or were interviewed.

There's me.
Then there's the other me who's
looking after the child.

Motherhood – a work in progress

Maggie Gordon-Walker
Founder of Mothers Uncovered

I usually cite my experiences in the first year of motherhood as the reason for setting up Mothers Uncovered. The feelings of isolation and loneliness, the sense that I was invisible behind my baby, the struggle I had between wanting my old life back and not wanting to be apart from my child. When probed, most new mothers will have an experience somewhere on the sliding scale between exhilaration and despair, often on a daily basis.

In fact, it was in pregnancy that I realised that this baby was bigger than the both of us (or not, as they thought). I knew exactly the night I'd conceived, but at my 12-week scan, my baby looked bigger than expected. They brought my due date forward by six days, and I went along with it, because you assume the professionals know better.

It wasn't until nearly six months later, at 37 weeks pregnant, that the midwife who put the tape measure across my bump at a routine check thought it was fractionally too small, more like a 36-week bump. Should she refer me to the hospital for a further scan? Why didn't I pipe up that instant? In truth, I had forgotten about the due date change – it seemed lost in the past and I'd slept badly throughout my pregnancy, meaning I wasn't particularly sharp by this point. So those last few weeks were spent toiling up to the hospital every two or three days. Each time, baby sounded fine on the monitor; each time, the scan produced nothing untoward; each time, they insisted I must come back again, the subtext being I would be harming my baby if I didn't. The busy London hospital was some

Photo: Kerry Ghais

miles away, with no parking, so the journey was a mammoth effort.

The juggernaut of the system

I escaped induction by a hairsbreadth. 'It's time to get this baby out,' declared a male doctor I'd never met before, striding into the appointment room. As if I was a blocked pipe. I suddenly remembered the due date change and declared excitedly that I was in line with what was expected. The juggernaut of the system was, by that point, too far gone. My words fell on deaf ears. I burst into tears, but he remained implacable. I pleaded for another day or two, which was reluctantly granted. I was given two sweeps, amongst mutterings that baby might not be growing properly. They predicted a birthweight no bigger than 6lb. Eventually, I started labour on my original due date, and my 7lb 7oz boy was born, already too big for the teeny sleepsuits I'd acquired.

This is far from the worst story about birth I, or any of us, have heard. I realise it was a minor problem, and myself and my baby were well and healthy, so the violins can be put away. There are many women and/or babies who might have died without intervention, so I am not knocking the system, which does a fabulous job a lot of the time. But the simple fact is, I wasn't listened to. I was the inconvenient and troublesome gated house to the treasure that lay within.

A daunting bundle of joy

Often, mothers are presented as greedy, demanding, or ungrateful; but, most of the time, all they want is to be heard. We believe we know what mothers think, because they're always being represented in the media. It is full of opinions about motherhood, little jibes about the categories of mother: 'career bitches', 'yummy mummies', 'hippies breast-feeding their children into adulthood'. There is an assumption that the day is filled by checking out the latest gossip on Mumsnet Towers and a spot of lunch, with a few nappy changes here and there. Posts on Instagram aside, very little

is written by mothers detailing their life in that first year. It is recorded retrospectively, if at all. This is mostly because it can get to 2.00pm before a new mother can find the time to brush her teeth.

There are however, many things written about mothers, often by those who are not mothers. Some, such as Bibi Lynch, in 'Mothers Stop Moaning', suggest that mothers are treated as superior citizens. As anyone who has battled with a baby in a busy place will tell you, this is not always the case. People tend to look the other way and tut when a noisy baby and harassed mother cross their path. Lynch was asked to get off a bus for a mother with a pram. Yes, that's not fair. Perhaps the woman might have been someone like me, who had cried every day since giving birth four months earlier. I'd been told I could only get on the bus if I folded the pram. The crowded bus watched as I tried to fold it with one arm, the other holding the baby, before admitting defeat and leaving the bus. Upset and very late for the group I was headed to, I phoned my partner, then didn't put my phone away properly. It was stolen. I didn't make it to my destination.

Some believe that mothers should just put up and shut up because this is what they have chosen. Yes, this is true, in the main, and complaints by mothers can understandably be seen as intolerable to women not able to have children. It is good, considering our over-populated planet, that not all women are mothers; but if everyone chose not to be mothers, then the world would end. Simples. Who will staff the hospitals, the supermarkets, the police, except for those children grown up? This 'us and them' attitude does nobody any favours. Women usually know how lucky they are to be mothers, and repeatedly deny any of their own needs until they are often in a desperate state. Yes, they have the immense gift of that baby; but to suggest that they should have no further sadness, anger or boredom in their lives, just because they are mothers, is preposterous.

Nobody expected bringing up children to be a breeze and, yes, we have been doing it for centuries; but there is something about a

> I am not knocking the system, which does a fabulous job a lot of the time. But the simple fact is, I wasn't listened to

mother's state of mind in the months following the birth, hit by the huge sense of responsibility, that sets it apart from the challenges faced later on in parenthood. It's hard to admit that you are finding so difficult what every mother did before you. That this longed-for bundle of joy should be so daunting. Add to this the stigma that still exists around mental health issues, and it's no wonder the feeling of panic can set in. The Association For Post-Natal Illness estimates postnatal depression affects up to 100,000 women and babies each year. Those are the reported figures; the truth is probably more.

Occasionally, there is a high-profile case where the public can gasp at the horror of a woman who has killed her own child. There is far less coverage for a mother who has taken her own life. More than 10% of maternal deaths – that's deaths within one year of giving birth – are caused by suicide. This doesn't even include suicides that come later, in some cases much later. In 2000, a mother from Cheshire laid down in front of a train because she had never recovered from the depression that started with the birth of her 24-year-old son.

Normalising despair
There is still an insistence on dividing mothers into those with 'baby blues' (perceived as the vast majority), from those with PND, postnatal depression (perceived as a small proportion). The latter are usually treated with medication and specialist counselling. These women are kept apart, in 'closed groups'. It's as if they fear that they might 'infect' the other mothers. There is a shaming stigma of 'not coping'.

It is imperative that this period, with its rollercoaster of emotions, is reclassified as 'normal' rather than 'extreme'. Some will have PND and need treatment. But every mother I have spoken to in the last few years has felt they couldn't find an adequate outlet for their feelings at the beginning. Were they all suffering from depression? On some days they wanted to celebrate how much they loved being a mother and share that with others. They didn't want to describe themselves as

If the right support were there in the first place, I firmly believe a lot of women would not develop PND

depressed then. Both the terminology and the attitude to this period of motherhood is wrong.

I am proposing the term 'New Motherhood Syndrome', in which it is perfectly normal to be blissfully happy one moment and in the depths of despair the next. If the right support were there in the first place, I firmly believe a lot of women would not develop PND.

Playing catch-up
What I would like to see is equal weight being given to the postnatal period as the pre-natal. The mental health of a mother following a birth is as important as her physical health beforehand. It's not even as if mothers want so very much. A supportive group, with some tea and biscuits. It's not exactly the moon on a stick, is it?

Anyone who thinks feminism no longer has a place needs to wake up and smell the testosterone. For example, Caroline Criado Perez, who campaigned for Jane Austen to feature on the £10, was treated as the devil incarnate on social media. Every day brings fresh horrors of this sort, even in the #metoo era. So, in my own small way, I am more determined than ever that mothers' voices should not be silenced. Not all women are mothers, but all mothers are women; and whenever they put their collective head above the parapet, they get it slapped back down.

Like so many women, I gradually realised that I was just a normal mother trying to cope with the enormity of the responsibility with inadequate preparation. That in turn put the feelings in proportion. I had a relatively mild case of depression (I suppose – I was never diagnosed), which lifted in time. Most women do just 'get on with it' and the memories of that turbulent time fade. By the time they re-enter the fray, they may find it hard to even remember that time clearly and may well not wish to, feeling thankful that they seem to have survived relatively intact. This is why the problem still continues. As a society we should offer more, especially when the support is easily achievable. And for the women whose lives are permanently blighted by their experiences of becoming a mother, the situation must change.

The article I wrote for The Guardian:
www.theguardian.com/commentisfree/2014/jul/08/health-system-failing-new-mothers-postnatal-depression-nhs

change.org petition:
www.change.org/p/public-health-england-nhs-mothers-need-more-support-help-them-now

mothersuncovered.com

There's not a real pivotal point when I've thought I'm a mum, but when my mum or dad calls me 'mum', it brings it home to me.

The big recognition comes when you have to fill in a form. When you write 'mother' for the first time.

Mother. Me.

How did that happen?

1. Anticipation

Can anything prepare you for having a baby?

The answer, in short, is 'no'. Mothers tend to find it difficult to communicate what it's like to have children; expectations barely ever match reality, and some don't think you should even try to tell a pregnant woman what will happen next.

At Mothers Uncovered sessions, we often ask women to write a postcard to their pre-pregnancy self, and most relish the opportunity to tell themselves everything they found it too difficult to hear at the time, or were never told. As U says, 'Even though you think, "Oh there's going to be sleepless nights; it's going to be tough," you're just not prepared for that exhaustion.'

Can anything prepare you for having a baby? You don't want to hear – you'll be so tired, it hurts…
From 'Your Stories'

You prepare only for birth
I didn't really realise how full-on it would be being a mum. Pregnancy: you spend your time – or I did, and I think this is true of a lot of mums – preparing for the birth, and everything hinges on that due date; you're building up and slowly getting closer to that date; you're doing all your preparations; then it comes and it goes; you have your baby suddenly; it's like, 'I've just spent nine months preparing and it's a six-hour event, and I've got a baby to care for – for the rest of my life.'
Interview with P, daughter 9 months

You can't tell women the truth
I don't think you could ever tell a pregnant woman the 'truth' – it wouldn't be fair. I remember walking along the seafront in the early months pushing a pram. I could catch the eye of any other mother and we would smile knowingly. It was almost like a secret club. Only you and they knew what a crazy, intense, demanding, lonely, amazing, tiring time you were having right at that moment. These shared looks were, it felt, almost a nod to solidarity in the face of this enormous un-talk-about-able challenge.

The most amazing aspect of being a mother is, perhaps, the extreme privilege of having a healthy child, to be able to hang out with that child, and to feel so much love, and to laugh and smile so much – this is completely precious and unique.

The biggest challenge is marrying up these overwhelming feelings with the mundane and, dare I say it, bored feelings that can slip in from time to time. It is sheer hard work – every day. As women, we are all so different; it is quite hard to imagine how a friend who is about to have a baby will feel and cope. So, overall, I would be very positive and encouraging to anyone about to become a mother, because that's all they need to hear at that moment!
Saskia Neary, from 'Your Stories'

If I met a stranger who was pregnant, I'd say, 'Congratulations, you look well, when's it due?' I don't think you could say the good and bad of

Photo: Cécile Chevalier

it, I just don't think I could say all that. I'd say to a pregnant friend, 'Good luck,' because you can be more honest with them. 'And get some sleep because you're not going to have any more for the next 18 years. Get a tough skin because you're going to get insulted and contradicted on everything you do now.'
Interview with B, daughter 15 months

It's never what you expect

It's a shame we are so judgmental about parenting and motherhood. I thought I'd be really 'attachment parenting' all the way, 'organic-bread-child', breastfeeding until she's 20. I felt really down on myself when I realised I couldn't give that much. I'm just starting to forgive myself about that. I'd really got my head round it and I felt like I was really prepared: I'd done lots of reading, lots of research; I felt like I was clear in how I wanted to bring her up, the things I wanted to do. I knew I wanted to breastfeed and I was really going to try, and I was so shocked by the difficulties. I just wasn't expecting them because you're not told about them.
Interview with K, daughter 8 months

At the airport on the way from my home country, two girls were sitting next to me in the waiting room talking. They were both au pairs. One said, 'When I'm going to be a mummy, I'm going to dress in nice clothes every day and I'm going to be a 'yummy mummy' – they used the English words. I listened, and after a while I started to smile and I couldn't bear to listen any more. I turned to her and said, 'Look, I have got a 14-month-old at home. If I spent all my money on lovely clothes, she'd spoil it all with her food and stains. If you want to do that, congratulations.' She was surprised.

I said, 'You'll be pleased when your baby is born that you can stay in your pyjamas for the first months. And be really privileged when you put on nice clothes, like jeans – whatever fits you. And you can go out for half an hour's walk.' I had to tell them it's not like that in normal life.

To a pregnant friend, I would say black and white, such as everything bad about pregnancy that I experienced: pain, feeling uncomfortable, heartburn, not being able to give birth to her (I had a caesarean). Don't believe in books; don't

believe anything that is written because it's not about you, it's about an average person. Good things: it may be the first moment you look into your baby's eyes. Listen to advice, because advice shouldn't be taken as an offence.
Interview with H, daughter 16 months

You read books and think your newborn baby will sleep 18 hours day; I thought I'd have lots of time to myself – 'I'll do my yoga practice while my baby's asleep' – and it's not like that at all. So I guess that was one of the things I was quite shocked about – that actually, in those early weeks, just finding time to go for a wee is just… you can't necessarily do that all the time. But it gets easier, and it has got easier; and it gets more enjoyable day by day as she develops her little personality, and it's great – you get so much back.
Interview with P, daughter 9 months

I don't know if motherhood was what I expected – probably a mix of 'yes' and 'no'. I think, as much as I felt like I was prepared, I guess I probably wasn't completely. Not just prepared for physical things, but mentally prepared as well. Even though you think, 'Oh there's going to be sleepless nights; it's going to hard; it's going to be tough,' you're just not prepared for that exhaustion. I was very lucky that I had a very easy pregnancy – I didn't have any sickness or complications, and I really enjoyed being pregnant.
Interview with U, son 6 months

Adding sperm to the cart
I've been with my partner for 12 years. I'm in a gay relationship, so it took a long time to work out how exactly things would work. We had an anonymous donor from a sperm bank. We've got a recording of his voice, so I think he's American. You sort of buy a package – it's like going on Amazon: you buy the sperm, then as many other options as you want; you add items to your cart. We got the lot, because we thought it would be her decision if she wanted to know more when she's older. It took just over a year from buying the sperm to her being born.
  I was scared of giving birth, but it was ok.

But I'd do it again. We've got more sperm; we'd like her to have full siblings. It creeps up on you, motherhood – you realise you've changed a lot.
Interview with M, daughter 9 weeks

Don't take anything for granted
I do have a habit of not fully thinking things through before I do them, like not reading a guidebook before I go on holiday. I really enjoyed being pregnant and wasn't really thinking past that. I had a miscarriage; then I had spotting when I was 11 weeks pregnant with her, so I wasn't taking anything for granted. Every milestone was a milestone.
Interview with I, daughter 4 months

Go your own way
Rather than following a routine or listening to baby experts, I'd rather do things in a baby-led way – so I watch what's going on with her and then respond to it. There was a point at which I thought, 'I'm going to do things my way, and ignore what the books, society and other women are saying. I can understand her, and I'm going to listen to myself.' Everything started getting a lot easier from then on. You have to be assertive because there are so many people telling you how you should do things. Before having a child, I wasn't particularly assertive – it's like she's given me motivation, because it's so important to me to get it right.
Interview with S, daughter 8 months

Do one thing in a day
My goals on a daily basis are different, because trying to achieve anything as you used to do is impossible – the day can just drift by. You can aim to do one thing in a day, I find. I've also had big to-do lists, doing stuff all the time, and I realised putting that extra pressure on myself wasn't worth it.
  It's not been easy. It's taken me a long time. I've realised that, 'Today I'm going to clean the bathroom – and that's it.' That's all I expect, because we try to get out of the house once a day.
Interview with G, daughter 14 months

2. Birth

Pain, fear and ecstasy

No surprise that this is one of the longest chapters. We dedicate a session of every course to birth stories, and no two are alike. For some, it's a spiritual journey, made while high on endorphins. Ellen Stewart even felt 'Like when I had been dancing in nightclubs 10 years before.' But for too many, it's a time of frustration, of plans thrown out the window, of pain and fear. 'Suddenly I became very scared... It was already so intense, so overwhelming, I would not be able to continue like this for hours,' says Caren Fisher. 'I shouted and was angry, as I desperately wanted a private space,' says an anonymous writer.

But the joy in their children shines through in the end. Saskia Neary talks about a loss of control that many women feel, but then sums it up: 'Once you have your baby, it doesn't really matter any more.'

I was rushing, loved-up

I remember it as a wonderful magical experience – it sits outside any other experience I've had – unique and bizarre. A place where time stops for 48 hours. Just for us, the world stopped for Tony and I, so we could bear our son. So I must have already forgotten the pain; it's already blurred at the edges, my body has forgotten the sensation. I remember being scared of every single contraction, though, and 14 hours in, thinking it would never end. I just wanted to stop and sleep – there was no way I was ever going to push this baby out. I remember, between contractions, being in total bliss: lying in the birth pool; the room being flooded with light, with huge windows; gazing at the midwife and the student, being held from behind by Tony.

I was rushing on pure endorphins, loved-up like I had been dancing in nightclubs 10 years before.

His arrival was just utter exhaustion, bewilderment, shock, disorientation. Here was this huge battered and bruised baby, lying across my breast, peering out of swollen eyes at me. I got them to give me a copy of the notes of the birth. It's quite amazing for looking back at, to see what happened. I think it's more moving than what I've penned. This is what was written: 'Delivery of live male infant. Delivered on to mother's abdomen. Dried, stimulated, cried at birth. Clean towel, cord clamped, cut by Tony. Baby skin to skin with mother, placed across breast.'
Ellen Stewart, from 'Your Stories'

I plunge and plunge until she is here

Crossing the seafront road, we pass Henry Allingham – First World War survivor and the world's oldest man – leaving in his funeral hearse. In two hours' time she will arrive.

At the lowest, most impossible point, when I absurdly, mulishly say, 'I can't do it, I can't,' the quiet, watchful midwife, with the beautiful cow-brown eyes speaks: 'I see lots of dark hair. Feel.' I reach down into the pool and feel –

between my legs, the clotted tendrils of her hair float free. It feels the way seaweed feels, brushing my legs when I swim. Now, everything is certain.

I plunge and plunge, and I'm the only one there until she is here; I grip her greasy duck-down body, her head above the water between my breasts, and look into an open howling mouth at some hardy gums.

Curiously, the first thought I have is: 'That is where her teeth will be.' And I think what I meant was – in that shocked moment – 'She will eat. She will speak. She will laugh. She will sing. She exists.'

Anna Kisby, from 'Your Stories'

There was no happiness when she was born

At the beginning, we were in hospital for quite a while. She was in the baby unit at the Royal Sussex. She wasn't 'there' at all and was completely unresponsive. It was really tough. When you're pregnant, you have the worries of 'What if you don't make it to the end?' and you don't think about beyond the birth, because it might go wrong. So when she was born, and it looked like she wasn't going to make it, I just thought, 'This is what I expected all along.'

I had a normal labour: she got a bit stuck, but it was pretty straightforward and I went into labour naturally. She'd obviously got into distress; to be honest, I think there was a fault on the side of the hospital, as they left it a bit long with giving help. So I had a very long second-stage labour, and I think she just got too tired, and it was all too much for her. We weren't aware, until she was being born, that something was wrong, as her heartbeat was fine – it was only at the very end. I can see those two things are definitely linked.

There was no happiness when she was born. When I think about it, it doesn't make me happy, it makes me feel really, really sad. And that was the exact opposite of how I expected. I thought it would be the happiest day of my life, and it just wasn't.

It gets easier, definitely; I can talk about it now without getting really upset, and I think about it objectively: she's obviously fine and

she's an easy baby. And the two things don't really go. On the one hand, there's this worry, worry, worry in my head; on the other hand, she's absolutely fine and there's nothing wrong with her. She's been really good; I was really surprised by that, as I really psyched myself up for massive disruptions. Whatever you expect, the opposite happens!

Interview with R, daughter 6 months

Not all bodies are made to give birth

LittleOne made his appearance a week before his due date. He must have heard me when I said I was ready, because he spared me another week of pregnancy and was born very quickly.

It was a very different experience from the first. I had a sweep at the hospital, and the waters broke. The day after, I woke up with mild contractions. I had an appointment at lunchtime for a check, and possibly an induction of labour. The consultant performed another sweep, and, less than two hours afterwards, I was in labour spontaneously – no time for pain relief other than gas and air, and the baby was born that afternoon.

It was brutal, but at the same time I was aware of everything and somehow more in control. I stayed off the bed as much as possible, and gravity really made a difference – the first time I gave birth, it was after a long initial stage – I got there already exhausted and had an epidural. Things went a lot more slowly, and I was in bed the whole time. This time, I had asked for an epidural; but when the doctor came in and asked me to sit still for a while, I just couldn't. And I couldn't stay on the bed. Suddenly, all the things I learned at the NCT classes – about the breathing, visualisations and positions during labour – made sense.

LittleOne was born. I had a heavy haemorrhage at the end, so the last stage was 'actively managed', which meant that I had to stay in bed and had an IV drip, while the doctors tried to stop the blood; but I also had a little perfect baby in my arms and didn't care. We stayed at the hospital for a few days, to make sure there wasn't any infection and that we were both well. I recovered quite well

Photo: Kerry Ghais

without the need for a transfusion, and every day I felt better.

The pelvic pain that had made me miserable throughout my pregnancy was gone, and I could stand on one leg again (you don't know what you have until you lose it, believe me); the stitches healed well; the baby was well, and I breastfed him. For a while, I still had lower back pain, and my wrists were sore where I had had the IV needle; but I was convalescent, after all.

Here was my little baby, and he seemed so fragile and defenceless; but at the same time, he had had the strength to stay alive through an IVF cycle, to wait in a freezer for four years, and to grow and come to this world, despite everything. And I'm amazed at what science and medicine have done for us, because people say that women's bodies are made to give birth, but that's not true for everyone: in my case, there were a few significant steps when the process would have failed or I would have had serious complications.

Chiara Corrao

I thought I'd have a water birth

The birth was a shock, in the sense that I wasn't expecting him then. I had convinced myself that I'd be one of those people who would be waiting around for ages. I was still working – I'd been working till midnight that week – and I was very stressed about work. They were saying, 'We know you're pregnant and you've got a week to go,' but at the same time, 'You've got to get this done.' I was lucky, I was home as it was a Sunday. I'd literally woken up from a sleep in the middle of the day and had period-type pain, and I thought I was getting Braxton Hicks as it was really sudden. I didn't have my waters break, but I actually started to bleed; that's when I really panicked, as I thought I was having a miscarriage.

We rushed in and I gave birth within three hours, which was completely the opposite to a lot of friends who've had really long and difficult births. I had no time for pain relief, just some gas and air.

He was 6lb 8oz, and he did look a bit premature and a bit jaundiced, but he would have been really big if he'd come on time. I didn't want to have any pain relief, really; but I never vetoed it as I didn't know how bad the pain was going to get.

I thought I'd have a water birth, but I was very conscious of the fact that no one I'd known had had the birth they thought they'd have. And I'd chosen Haywards Heath, but we were in Brighton.

I had to have him on the table, and I really felt like kneeling down on the floor; but, because he was premature, they were monitoring him. But I managed to be on my side, and it wasn't too restrictive. I'd done yoga, but I was in such a panic I didn't breathe very well until right at the end.

I managed to deliver the placenta naturally, as well. He was on my stomach, and that was an amazing moment. I couldn't believe I'd given birth to a baby. I had this vision of him being inside as a foetus. When he came out, I was thinking, 'Oh my god, you have hair and everything.'

Even when he was born, I kept thinking, 'I need to be at work tomorrow,' as I was still in shock and I was thinking I was going to let them down.

I'm generally quite organised, but I hadn't done a birth plan. I'd half packed my hospital bag already, but only because I'd had a panic the week before. One thing I've really learned since having him, is you just have to let things go and do things at a different pace. It's not like at work, when you can get ten things done – that's a good life lesson; I really love being with him.

I'm usually really squeamish, and I once fainted in science class when they were explaining things like childbirth. It's weird, though – all the blood and everything didn't bother me at all as it felt completely right, and the placenta thing I wasn't worried about. I didn't want to get it over really quickly as I wanted as much blood as possible to get to him.
Interview with V, son 8 months

Very quick and easy
The birth was at the Royal Sussex, as planned, and an enjoyable birth. It was very straightforward – very quick and easy. I don't

quite know why. It was painful but it wasn't unbearable. When I went full term and gave birth, I had a feeling of euphoria that came over me. I suppose again it might have been the hormones that kicked in. I got to the hospital at 4.20am and he was born at 6.42am, so 2 hours 22 minutes in labour. It started at about 2.00am, and I didn't realise what it was as it didn't feel how I thought it would.

It felt like period pains, and I just thought I kept needing to go to the loo; it finally clicked by 4.00am, and I went in. It was three days before the due date. I wasn't working and he saw his opportunity to come out: 'She's not at work, I'd better come now before she gets back in there.'

I was quite serene. My sister came, and she was there when he was born. Apparently, I didn't make any noise and just had him. It was mainly because I was really worried that so many of my friends had had caesareans as they got really tired; I didn't want that to happen, so I'd thought, 'I'm going to conserve as much energy as I can.' I think, regarding his birth, I just trusted my instincts with it, and it seemed to work. I took a practical attitude towards it and thought, 'I've got to do this as quickly as I can.'

There was going to be a shift change, too, so I didn't want to start with one midwife and finish up with another. So I kind of took control of it and just decided. The midwife said to me, 'I probably won't be here when you're actually giving birth,' and I thought, 'No I'm not having that.' When I went in, I was 5cm dilated. So I did most of it at home with two paracetamol. I had gas and air when I went in.
Interview with Q, son 4 months

It's not a boy!
When I was 20 weeks' pregnant, we had a scan. There was a trained nurse in the room with her back to us, and we asked her if she could say what the sex of the baby was. She turned the monitor towards us and said, 'There are the little testicles, so it's a boy,' because she saw three little things. We were

over the moon because in the whole family there were no grandsons yet, only granddaughters. I thought I was going to be the first mummy of a boy. We got everything ready for a boy, even the day I went into labour my partner went out and bought a card and a blue balloon. All the cards were given to us beforehand for a baby boy. I even made video diaries at home talking to him.

When she came out, it was shocking. The whole day was really shocking because I had had dreams about giving birth in a relaxed environment at home with my partner's support. When I couldn't cope with the pain any longer and she turned breech, we had to go to hospital and she was born by C-section. When I was in the hospital, I had a funny feeling that she wasn't a boy.

The doctor said he couldn't tell because she had so much meconium that her whole bottom was covered. From that point, I told my partner, 'I don't think I can deal with not having a boy.' He said, 'Don't worry, does it really matter?'

I said to the doctor, 'Please tell me it's a boy,' and he said, 'No, it's a girl.' I was completely disappointed. I know it's not really nice, but I had a dream to have a boy. I didn't get anything out of the birth that I wanted: it wasn't a home birth, it wasn't a natural birth, and it was a girl. I was told it had to happen that way because it was me, because everything in my life happens like this. Everything turns out good in the end. I would not change her for anything. Even a few days after she was born, I said that I was so pleased to have a girl.
Interview with H, daughter 16 months

Her first few days
The side room was small. It was hot and bright, giving some sense of the summer occurring outside. It felt airless, but once the window that ran the width of the room was opened only slightly, it soon became too draughty; comfort couldn't be achieved there. Or, rather, her comfort was no longer the issue. It was, however, a very welcome upgrade from the curtained bay on the ward,

where she had felt herself nearly explode with exposure.

The baby with the yellow skin lay on the BiliBed next to the window, masked like a little Zorro, naked but for a nappy, bathing in illumination. She looked far too content, like she had regressed to an in utero state. She kicked her soft ankles and twisted her toes occasionally as if easing her feet into the sea… the alarming lights seemed incongruous to the blind tranquillity beneath them.

The mother sat on the bed, wide-eyed and wired, displaced from herself already. Seagulls stalked the roof outside the window. If she couldn't touch or hold the child constantly, or be seen, then she would talk continually. Thus she maintained an earnest stream of consciousness, providing the room and her companion with a constant narrative to allay her grief.

The sad rhythm of the breast pump filled the room periodically. Sticky, lanolin grease stains met her one and only feeding top repeatedly. A pile of fresh fruit and a water jug were replenished as regularly as she gratefully exploded with iron-rich shit in the ensuite. Vivid iodine-swelling marked the hand and wrist where a stranger's blood had entered her. Regular visitations were received from professionals, with their concerned tones, and careful consultation of charts and levels.

One afternoon, a seagull seemed to stand a lively guard over the child. With her mind free to indulge itself somewhat, she supposed it was Crazy Lolly, with whom she had made memorable light of the seagull life just before she moved down to the sea, not long before Lolly took her own flight – a marvellous woman seen off too young by rogue ovaries. She grinned at the old bird thankfully, before musing on the new enormity of her own mortality.

As she let down milk, she felt sudden surges of oxytocin that bewildered her and induced a sinister sleepiness, at odds with the click of the cleaner's sweep against the bed. When allowed to release the child for feeding, she kissed her sweet face and head, inhaling her scalp and clutching her close like a life jacket. This must be the place, she said.
Claire Robinson

There was no way I could move

It was approximately 11.00am when my midwife arrived. She came straight into the bathroom to try to gently coerce me out of the bath water. There was no way I could move – I was not able to get up. I wanted to stay in the water, it felt like mercy. I knew the baby was coming soon; I needed to stay in the water; I needed to push.

'You need to relax, dear. Your baby is not coming for some time yet. If you get out of the bath, I will be able to examine you to see how things are progressing.'

I could not believe it. Her words cut straight through my confusion. Suddenly, I became very scared. If this was the early latent phase, then I knew I would certainly not be able to cope with the later stages of labour. It was already so intense, so overwhelming, I would not be able to continue like this for hours.

Eventually, I was able to stand, and, leaning heavily on G's strength, I walked over to the bedroom and lay down. I was crying and deflated as I opened my legs for her to examine me. I needed to calm myself down, to find a way to get through the early phase of labour. Perhaps I had been overconfident to believe that I was capable of getting through childbirth at home, with no interventions other than breathing and love. I began to have doubts, to wonder if I was strong enough to cope.

G and I had decided to try for a home birth. We spent the weeks leading up to the birth attending antenatal workshops, preparing ourselves physically and mentally to cope with the arrival of our baby. We wanted to share the experience in the comfort and safety of our flat. We bought a birth pool, prepared the bedroom for resting. We were excited, but relaxed. I was jittery with third trimester nerves, while G remained outwardly calm and level-headed. After all, first babies are always at least ten days later than their due date. We knew we had lots of time to prepare to buy all the necessary bits and pieces.

So, without concern, we went to bed in the comfort and knowledge that we had time. We would go out to buy nappies and a blanket later that week. We would test out the pool some time tomorrow, and possibly even go out for drinks with some friends that evening. For these reasons, when I woke on the next morning with cramps, I was sure I had constipation.

It was quite a surprise when we both finally realised that the cramps were minutes apart and I was in labour. At 7.00am, the process had begun. By 9.30am, I was unable to move. I rocked on the bed, hugging my knees with my head in G's lap. We were confused – it was all happening so quickly.

We finally decided to ring the maternity ward to give them the coordinates. Needless to say, they calmly suggested I take two paracetamol and go for a walk or soak in a hot bath. And that is how I came to be stuck in a cold, shallow bathtub for an hour and 45 minutes.

G called for a midwife to come and help because he was unable to keep count of the contractions. As my birthing partner, he was tasked with the important job of keeping count. As my soulmate, he was my strength, the keeper of the space. Ready to solve, ready to count contractions, ready to light the candles, burn the essential oils, fill the pool, monitor the temperature. He was ready to hold me up, lay me down, ready to speak for me, to sing for me, or leave for me if I called for it. However, it just so happened that, at that point, he was not quite ready for what happened next.

Through gritted teeth, I demanded that he 'Get someone who knows what the fuck is going on.' And that is how the midwife came to my rescue.

To my infinite relief, after the internal examination, I recall her voice uttering words to G I shall never forget: 'Here are my car keys. Please fetch my bag, and be quick – the baby is coming now!' I was ten centimetres dilated and the baby was ready to be born.

There was no time for the pool; no time for candles, oils or music. I manoeuvred to the floor, leaned against G and helped the baby birth on dry land. By 12.47pm, she was born; by 1.47pm, the placenta was out.

Caren Fisher, from 'Your Stories'

They looked exasperated with me

I remember feeling happy and calm at home that sunny morning. My partner hadn't left for work when the contractions started, so he was home and we got ready together as we waited for my mum to come to be with our elder daughter. We have a lovely photo of the three of us and my bump before saying goodbye, and we're all glowing with excitement. We drove to the hospital and I timed myself through the contractions in the back of the car, using that as a focus to help me get through each minute.

I had to explain to the lady over the check-in desk that my waters had broken three days earlier, that I'd been checked over and was on oral antibiotics, that I'd wanted to have a gentle home birth but now wasn't allowed one as baby was a month early, that I wanted to be taken to the home-from-home area in the hospital and not the medicalised area, that I didn't want to be hooked up to any drips or have to lie on a bed with no movement, and ideally I wanted to be in water for relaxation and pain relief. I said my contractions were very regular and close, and that baby would probably be here any moment.

They said I would categorically not be allowed in the home-from-home area, so I explained that I had spoken to a doctor and a consultant midwife in the last few days about my wishes, and could they try to contact her/find my notes, please? I think they asked me to go and pee in a bottle, which I somehow managed to do through the contractions, and then wait for an assessment behind a curtain in a public area.

I was feeling more and more agitated, as I knew my baby was coming very soon and I wanted to be in a room to relax asap – so when they took my blood pressure, it was very high. They looked quite exasperated with me, as I was loudly professing that I wanted a room as baby was about to come, and I didn't want it to be born behind this curtain; but they appeared to be wanting to follow their procedures, and I wasn't allowed to leave the area as I hadn't finished my assessment and met all the criteria required. They gave me an internal examination and said they were surprised that

I was so dilated. That proved I was quite far along the birth process, as I thought, but I still couldn't go anywhere as my blood pressure was so high. I shouted and was angry, as I desperately wanted a private space; but I stood there, took a huge deep breath, controlled my entire body into stillness, and asked them to do the blood pressure again. At which point, it went down to normal. I shouted: 'Right then, is that what you needed to see? Now get me to a room now!'

I was walked along the corridor and arrived in a large, bright room full of sunshine with massive windows overlooking the Houses of Parliament. It was nice – but I didn't want to be in a huge bright space right now, and the room seemed to be filling up with people and equipment. I wanted to be private so I went into the windowless bathroom. Things were progressing very fast and the contractions were really close together. From nowhere, the consultant midwife appeared in person, and I was really calmed to have her presence and hear her voice. She was like an angel appearing in a sea of clinical madness.

Ten short minutes, and some painful but steady contractions passed. I suddenly needed a poo. And I was going to be sick and I had a massive urge to push – which to do first? The consultant midwife's voice calmly told me it was normal – it was just the baby coming – and to get down on all fours, which felt strange; but I trusted her voice and I did what she said. My head was down on the floor under the sink, in the corner of a grimy hospital toilet. I tried to ignore the bin next to me. I felt the need for one large push, and in one go – two hours and 10 minutes after my first contraction at home – my baby came shooting out of me to be caught by whoever was behind.
Anonymous

I felt like it was getting out of control

A classic story of planned home birth ending up in an emergency caesarean section. I had a really wonderful few days with my partner trying to bring on labour. My waters broke on the Sunday, and by the Wednesday, still nothing had happened. We went for windy spring walks on Shoreham beach and along the seafront in Hove, where a shipload of wood had just been dramatically washed up on the beaches. We had curry, pineapple, sex, jumping up and down, and acupuncture. Nothing happened.

The flat was spotless. The sitting room was one large bed. A pool had been borrowed but not set up.

I went into hospital for a check-up, and the doctor reacted very strongly indeed to the fact that we had left it so long since the waters broke. He wanted me to stay in and be induced immediately. I was quoted NICE guidelines and told I was risking the baby's health by waiting a moment longer.

Mike drove anxiously home to get my stuff. I waited in an empty room for him to come back, not knowing what would happen next. I didn't want to see the doctor again until Mike was safely there by my side. We had been wrapped up wonderfully in our little bubble for the last week and had suddenly been jettisoned into a harsh reality wake-up call.

To cut a long story short-ish, I had to have intravenous antibiotics straight away – either that or the baby would have to have them when born, they said. Whoever put the line into my hand messed it up twice, and I ended up with a very swollen, painful hand, which I could not then use, and a line in the other. I was given a pessary, and I went into labour all night long – or so I thought – but many hours later they said I had not dilated at all. So all the energy and pain of that long night had been for nothing. This felt quite demoralising for both of us and a bit confusing.

The midwife who had introduced herself to us at the very beginning of this long night we never saw again. Another popped her head in at one point and then didn't come back for hours. I called for the person in charge in the early hours of the morning, because I felt like they were really mucking me about. Mike had gone to get gas and air, and it never arrived. I was in a lot of pain and no one came – etc etc. I could hear other women in the ward howling in pain.

Everyone was seemingly rushed off their feet and, no doubt, doing their utmost to deal with everyone's needs. However, I was starting to feel like my situation was getting out of control.

At some point, they decided to take me to another room and give me an epidural. I remember the very young women who administered the line to my spine. She was very confident and reassuring, and did it well and efficiently. This was Thursday by now. Labour followed; I had more lines put into my hand. I had to lie on my back the whole time, but it was fine – I was pretty out of it and felt no pain. Several more midwives came and went.

I remember the epidural wearing off because they had to take the line out for some reason and they forgot to put it back in – suddenly I was in the full-blown pain of labour. I remember the female doctor in charge taking a look and telling me the baby's head was turned. I had an hour more, she said, to try and turn the head before they would try forceps or go to a caesarean. All this time the baby's heart rate was fine – so I never felt worried about the safety or wellbeing of the baby. I had my mum and Mike with me. They were great, although distressed with the whole scene.

In the end, I was taken in for an emergency caesarean. I remember lying on my back and asking all the staff in the room to please be gentle with me and to do a really good job. I remember looking up at the female doctor at one point, and she had my blood up to her elbows and spatterings of it on her protective goggles. My baby girl was pulled out of me and she was fine. I was over the moon, and so was Mike.

Some staff had been great throughout, and some had been less than OK and had contributed to me feeling very vulnerable indeed. But overall, once you have your baby – and in my case she was healthy and everyone was fine – it doesn't really matter any more.

Saskia Neary, from 'Your Stories'

3. Breastfeeding

... and what they tell you

Guilt, shame, pride, nurturing love – so many feelings are aroused by breastfeeding, and not being able to breastfeed. If feeding your baby is the most natural thing in the world, why does it hurt so much and why is it so hard? 'My nipples felt like they'd had a cheese-grater on there,' says F. Or the time it takes can be overwhelming: U says, 'He'd be feeding and an hour later he'd be feeding again. I felt quite trapped in the early days.' The other side of the coin, of course, is mothers' happiness that they alone are sustaining their baby, and the close bond that brings. 'It can be quiet and blissful when they are feeding and you are comfortable,' says Ellen Stewart. Although we often had bottle-feeding mothers in our group, we sadly don't have any writing from them but we support all mothers' choices of how to feed their baby.

I hope we've formed a bond

My mum didn't breastfeed me. She said I was two months premature, she had asthma, and in the 70s they used to say don't breastfeed if you've got asthma. I don't know how true that is. That's made me think about my relationship with her. You have that bonding time when you're breastfeeding, which gives me hope that we've formed a good bond through feeding. It's such a special thing to do.

I remember talking to someone who said, when they wake up and feed, she thinks how many other mothers are doing the same thing; I do that sometimes now, which is a really nice thing to do. I've got friends whose babies wake up at a similar time and I occasionally think, 'Ah, there's loads of mums all round Brighton, all round the world right now doing the same thing.'

Interview with P, daughter 9 months

In the middle of the night is a new place, a new land, where I hadn't been that many times before Oscar. It can be lonely, and filled with anxiety, when you're incredibly tired. But it can also be quiet and blissful when they are feeding and you are comfortable. I remember looking for hours outside the windows of our front room to the houses opposite to see if any other lights were on – was anybody else up at 4.00am?

Ellen Stewart, from 'Your Stories'

Pain

With the breastfeeding, I had awful trouble with him for the first 11 weeks. He was premature, only by a month, but for the first six weeks I was constantly expressing and he couldn't feed. After that, I got a real breakthrough and I could use a nipple guard, and he managed to feed through that as it hits the back of their mouth and it causes the sucking reflex. But after a while, it became excruciating as he managed to grab on to the end of the nipple through the guard, and that created a kind of vacuum, and it was bleeding and everything, and I thought I'd never get the hang of it. I'd always wanted to breastfeed.

Interview with V, son 8 months

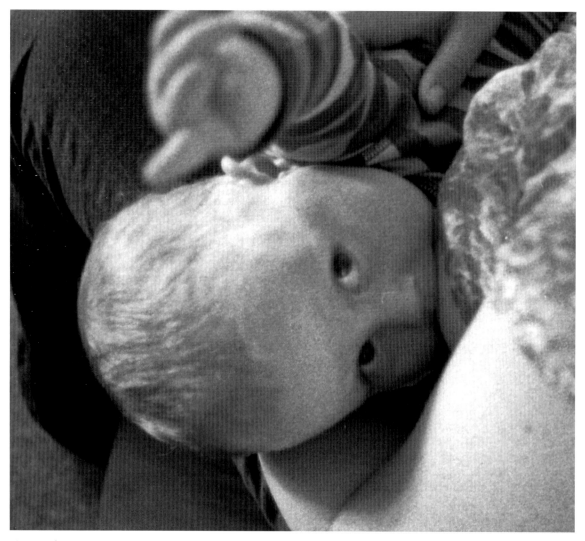

Photo: Cécile Chevalier

The feeding was really difficult the first six weeks because I was so sore. My nipples felt like they'd had a cheese-grater on there. I could so easily have given up. I did have a breastfeeding counsellor round – she was really good. It's just a slight thing with the positioning, the angle they're at – it can be a really minute little detail, you're so tired you hadn't taken it in. It did take about six to eight weeks to get it properly worked out, then the pain did go. It's just constant though, being not completely worn out so you've got the energy. I felt like I was cracking up at moments.
Interview with F, son 17 months

My baby was jaundiced in the first 24 hours, and so after our first night together in a private room, we were moved onto the ward and she had to lie in a lightbox to be treated. It was extremely noisy, with visiting families from around the globe singing praises to their new babies, people in different beds complaining to the staff about their care, or watching TV soaps on full blast and letting their toddlers run up and down shouting. I just wanted quiet and privacy for my new family.

My baby was floppy and sleepy with her illness, and didn't want to feed, so I ended up hand- (and later pump-) expressing and feeding her from a syringe, and then a cup. It was a massive learning curve and really stressful because, although I'd been to antenatal classes and knew that breastfeeding was healthy and supposedly straightforward, I was completely unaware of possible complications. I'd assumed babies just wanted to feed when they were born and our bodies would work together naturally to make that happen.

I became preoccupied with logging all of her feeds to be sure enough had occurred in each 24 hours, and trying to get her to latch on and take the milk. I was doggedly determined to carry on as I had never considered bottle feeding. The thought of giving my beautiful pure baby processed powdered milk dispensed through a plastic container was totally abhorrent to me, and therefore not an option. It was a huge battle to learn, gather information, find a diagnosis, and access treatment for each of the issues I encountered. The high stress levels of this time continued for the first three months of her life.

Through this period, I leaked copious amounts of milk day and night – it went all over the bed and my clothes. I was exasperated and crying out in pain at each feed. My nipples were cracked and bleeding, with continued blisters appearing. I also experienced excruciatingly painful thrush, which made me extremely sensitive to any kind of fabric on my breast area, and it felt like my chest was full of crunchy crushed glass when feeding. I had antibiotics for possible bacterial infection in my breasts, and had to be treated with other strong medications and creams for the thrush, which I would have rather avoided.

At the same time, I experienced equally painful vasospasms from Raynauds Syndrome in-between feeds. The blood flashed in and out of my nipples, and the pain was agonising. We found our daughter had tongue-tie, and we had to go through the long process of having her assessed and then the emotional procedure to have it cut. I was in and out of midwife-led support groups and doctor's appointments daily, but it took months to unravel what was happening. Towards the end, I saw a lactation consultant who was amazingly helpful as she understood my issues straight away, and her support was very reassuring.

After three months, we had answered all of the questions; the problems settled down and I relaxed. I fed my daughter until she decided to stop on her own, when my second baby was born 19 months later. When I think about breastfeeding, I can still feel the pain of all of these combined issues in my shoulders, and deep in my breasts and nipples, right now – seven years on.
Anonymous

I was conscious of being judged
There was so much guidance throughout my pregnancy. I was induced so I was in hospital five days before I actually had him – it was a long process. So there was all this support, but after I had him I remember being a bit lost and like, 'What do I do now?' because you're left to your own devices. Once we got home, I felt a bit more confident, more in control. In the hospital, I was probably a bit conscious of being judged. He didn't want to feed very much there and they put on a bit of pressure – they wanted to see him feeding before I went home. I wasn't worried about him, though. He was just really tired. But once we got home, he was feeding fine – it just happened naturally and I thought it would – I didn't want to force it.
Interview with U, son 6 months

A public affair
Breastfeeding took a little while to get the hang of, for both of us. I didn't know that I'd be able to do it in public and I thought I might feel awkward, but I don't feel awkward at all. There's so much going on in Brighton and lots of support, unlike some other areas.
Interview with Q, son 4 months

When he started feeding, it was a massive relief. I did feel a couple of times that it would have been easier to bottle-fed, but for me I wanted that closeness. With the nipple guard – that was brilliant – but I felt quite inhibited about things like going to the park. I got a breastfeeding apron initially, because I had the guard and it kept falling off. Now it's quite different, and I don't usually use it because he's usually quite good at feeding. I've used it a couple of times if he gets distracted. For example, like when we had to go to Australia it was great – he could just get under it; he fed all the way there and all the way back; he fell asleep under there, and he wasn't really distracted. Or if I'm in a restaurant, I'm more aware of how other people feel sometimes, so it's just easier. I did feel like it was never going to happen and I just wanted that tenderness with my child.

I had lots of help, but lots of conflicting advice. I felt like I was constantly getting my breasts out for everyone who came round, and you do get a bit tired of that. I'm quite stubborn, so I persevered. That's good now and it's really satisfying being able to provide for him. He's kind of gone the other way now and loves to feed, and it's probably why he had trouble sleeping.

He's been waking up four or five times a night to feed; but the last couple of nights, he only woke at 3.00am and 5.00am. He hadn't been doing that throughout – coming back from a visit abroad threw him quite a lot, as we got out of a habit.

We tried various things and wanted to try to do the gentle approach if possible. But he's got it now, and he loves to feed, it's like he's holding on to it.
Interview with V, son 8 months

I always think of breastfeeding as a complete nightmare. I didn't like the expressing, I felt like a cow – I should have had people yodelling behind me.
Interview with B, daughter 15 months

Challenges
I have flat nipples. My mother apparently does too, and was told firmly not to even try breastfeeding. I wanted to though and bought a contraption called a Niplette, a bizarre, medieval-looking suction tube that pulled the nipple out so the baby could latch on. In

Photo: Cécile Chevalier

theory. In practice, there was maybe ten seconds before the nipple retreated and if the baby bopped it with his head while trying to latch on, it was game over and you had to try again. Eventually my baby learned how to latch, but it was a challenging time.
Anonymous

Trapped
In the early days, so much feeding, not being able to leave him at all because he was so unpredictable in the early days. I had friends and their babies slept three or four hours, and they could go and do something. I couldn't do that as he'd be feeding and an hour later he'd be feeding again. I felt trapped in the early days. But it just got easier as he got older; around three and a half months. He slowed down with his feeding – that was quite gradual, I suppose – and became more predictable.

He went a bit longer and started sleeping longer at night. When he was about 15 or 16 weeks, he started sleeping through the night – well, 11.00pm till 7.00am – which is what he's done since then, so that's been amazing. In general, he's good with naps in the day and all that kind of thing.
Interview with U, son 6 months

4. Body image

Dramatic changes and new function

A change in body image is not just about the wear and tear of pregnancy and giving birth, or the extra weight many people put on; but a change of function, a sense that a woman's body no longer belongs just to her and has a practical use for another person. This can be a very positive experience, but some new mothers feel it contributes to their loss of a sense of self. G says, 'I feel like my body's a machine to service her. Pulling on clothes that are serviceable, not caring what I look like, just to run down to the shop.'

Quite like it. Flobberly and I don't give a shit about it.

Depressed – it isn't what it was – lumpy and bumpy. Your body is for your baby not for you.
From 'Your Stories'

Bodily integrity
I am a body.
A body that pushes two humans
and the wheeled weight of all their accompaniments
and paraphernalia
up hills, over kerbs, down steps and on to buses,
amid frowns, stares and some pitiful cares
as I stand so rudely, dishevelled in unchosen clothes
either too big or too small.
So visible, yet invisible, it seems.

A body that ballooned twice
and still inflates in rages
with blood boiling and occasional uterine agitation.
A body brazen in its disregard for delicacy.
A body that is home to a heart that persists,
with hands that faithfully grip.
A body that barely sits or shits
with bulbous veiny tits that itch
from hungry mewling scratching.
A body with wrists swollen from care
and a spine dutifully contorted
during the death of each day's life.
A body that pushed on two lives before they made breath
rendered now a suffocated perspiring mess.
A body that used to smoke and fuck
and stretch and rest and reach and saunter
that now creeps and creaks and folds;
that is merely mother to his daughters
no longer lover to covet or a hand to hold.
A body that walks and walks and rushes
with supposed purpose
in great strides of sweat as it bemoans
the injustice of the time all the while
like the White Rabbit.
A body that stinks so sweetly in its various folds
and pisses itself discreetly while it teaches
another poor female form the art
of wearing big girl knickers.
Claire Robinson

I enjoyed being large
When my bump grew, I loved my new look. I was waiting for hormone surges, but they never happened, I just felt really happy. Once I

gave birth, my boobs were huge, but everything else looked tired – the skin hasn't snapped back into place. My emphasis has been on my baby, though, so everything else is secondary to that.

Interview with L, son 7 months

I used to be a dancer so I was tiny and had quite a limited diet, but I'd put on weight before I was pregnant. My partner introduced me to things like pizza and curry. I really enjoyed being large when I was pregnant. Since I've had her, I've tried to become a healthy mum, incorporate more exercise. Now she's weaning, everything I eat she wants to eat, so I've weaned myself off the rubbish and have naturally started to lose the weight.

I've seen so many small children worry about their body image, so we don't say the 'f' [fat] word in our house – it has such a detrimental effect on their mental health. My body image is my issue, and it should remain insular. At first, I didn't like wearing the baby carrier I got because it split my tummy in half and I looked awful, but five months on I'm wearing it because that's what she likes. I'm self-aware because I know it'll impact her in some way.

Interview with E, daughter 9 months

My body image has changed, but I don't really care now. I hated the feeling after she was born, this wobbly brick-like feeling in my tummy, like tons of jelly. I thought it was never going to go away, it was just going to stay like that. I have quite a bit of loose skin on my tummy but I can hide it in clothes. I don't really care about stretch marks because I'm not going to show it off. I feel much more sexy now than when I had a flat tummy and I could wear bikinis.

Interview with H, daughter 16 months

I wasted 15 quid on knickers
A lot of women I spoke to found they didn't want to breastfeed because they didn't feel that comfortable with their new bodies in front of their partner. You've just had a baby so you should do, but your body changes so much. I put on four stone when I was pregnant. I can't

wear any of the clothes I did have. I just need a chainsaw. I don't know my sizes; I went into a shop to buy some underwear and I bought size 10,12,14,16 pants – I wasted 15 quid on knickers.

Interview with B, daughter 15 months

I can't have chocolates in the house
My body image is not very good. I've not helped matters because I eat too much. I do comfort eating because I'm not going out at the weekends. Saturday night is still Saturday night – I have a curry or a Chinese. I try not to have chocolates in the house, otherwise I'll wolf them down.

It's hard to do exercise because I've got him to look after. I did see a keep fit class for mums, but it's on a day I'm working. I used to go running – I did the half marathon twice. I wouldn't be able to walk into my old gym now – I'm just a blob. My tummy's not gone at all. Sometimes I look about five months pregnant. I couldn't wear a nice tight top. There are times I could do it – he goes to be with his dad on Saturdays – but there's always something like cleaning to be done.

Interview with F, son 17 months

I'm not interested in sex
I feel like my body's a machine to service her. I've never had body issues, but it's more to do with losing my sexual self – pulling on clothes that are serviceable, not caring what I look like, just to run down to the shop; not having time to think who I am, how I feel. I'd like to have more of a sense of myself. It affects my relationship with my partner because I'm not interested in sex. I feel like that sensual side of me has been lost at the moment.

Interview with G, daughter 14 months

It's amazing what your body can do
I'm quite happy with my body image, which is strange, but I've actually lost more weight than I gained during pregnancy from so much breastfeeding and carrying her. And I wasn't trying to lose weight or diet, so I'm quite pleased how that's worked out.

I enjoy breastfeeding – I enjoy that I can use my body to nurture her. It's like, this is what I'm here to do. I've always been quite anti-how women's bodies are presented in the media so it's nice to find something that is empowering, and a way I can use my body image positively. Although I understand that some women find breastfeeding difficult and have had different experiences, I think it's a great way to turn that around.

I've never been that happy with my body image in the first place. I was quite happy to be pregnant and I didn't mind, as I thought a pregnant body was a beautiful body. One big difference I noticed was I got really bad stretch marks under my breasts. It was only in the last two weeks, and if I'd carried him for the full nine months, I would have more. But, to be honest, I was really proud of what I'd done. I'm not a great exerciser, so if I'd made more effort, I'd have more reason to complain. Also, my job really took over before he was born, and I can actually do a lot more exercise now. I can't go off and do things without him but we're walking around town all the time. Now my stretch marks have actually faded a lot, and I think of them as my battle scars.

I feel a lot of pressure on women out there to look amazing. Being a mum, you realise everything isn't about you any more, it's like, 'Look what I've done.' Life is so much better with him to be worried about the odd stretch mark, although I feel a bit paranoid about them. In my NCT class, I meet up with five other mums every week. They're doing WeightWatchers, and they're dropping and

vanishing before my eyes, and are smaller than me now – it's not just my imagination. I guess, because I'm taller, other people are more petite; and some would see my height as a good thing, but I feel like maybe I stand out more.

I feel really ok with my body – I've never really had too much of an issue with how I look physically. I suppose I occasionally have doubts, but very fleeting – I'll a look in the mirror and think, 'Oh, that doesn't look too good,' and then it's gone. I've never had anything that's played on my mind. When I was pregnant, I did think, 'Oh, this is going to be interesting.' After I'd just had her, I remember not really feeling that my body had changed that much; but then I tried on some jeans and I couldn't even get them up past my thighs; and it's kind of hit me suddenly that I have actually put on quite a lot of weight. And I talked to friends who had had babies who said it was never the same.

But I looked in the mirror and felt I looked in proportion. Maybe it was just the realisation that my body's changed to have her, and it's quite different to putting on weight when you haven't had a baby. I'm still in awe of the fact that I grew her in my tummy and gave birth to her. So I think my body image is actually really good because of that, because it's amazing what your body can do. I see that my body is still nurturing her, feeding her. That's one of the things that blew me away, because I breastfed exclusively up to six months, and she grew just from my milk – I think that's fantastic.

 Sleep

Exhaustion colours everything dark

This is the one. The one that can most distort the experience of new motherhood. Sleep deprivation colours everything dark; and so many women find themselves shocked at how low they feel, how negative their mood is, when they feel they should be feeling happy to have a new baby. Which makes them feel worse. 'I was just too exhausted to enjoy it because it is draining; and I felt really guilty, thinking, "I've been looking forward to having this baby for ages," but I was just so tired,' says S. It can become an obsession: 'I fantasise about bed, a bed to myself – sleep sleep sleep,' says Anna Kisby. And even when it comes, it can be fleeting and uncomfortable. Kate Ballard says she loved co-sleeping, but that she got 'terrible backache from staying in the same awkward position on my side'.

The vortex of annihilation

Everyone told me while I was pregnant : 'Enjoy your sleep while you have the chance.' 'Yes,' I'd say, smiling politely, but inside my head I'd be screaming, 'I'm a fucking insomniac! Get lost!'

But – and I hate to say this – they were right. Even my pre-baby insomnia was better than the first 18 months of motherhood sleep. I've never known anything like the tiredness – dragging myself out of bed, full of cold with a whole day's work ahead of me, knowing I wasn't going to be able to do anything sensible; being woken up every hour to breastfeed – and I'd thought breastfeeding was going to be some kind of wondrous earth-mother experience. In the middle of the night, it did not feel like this. I found it impossible to sleep while breastfeeding – I remember lying on the living room floor and feeling as though I was being sucked into a vortex of annihilation. I know that sounds dramatic, but it was dramatic. It's not every day you feel yourself being forcefully sucked into the earth's core. Although it was every day for a while.
Megan Kendall, from 'Your Stories'

The fantasies

I fantasise about bed, a bed to myself – sleep sleep sleep – reading a novel lying in bed all day long, getting up for food carried back to bed – dreamy sleep, dozing sleep, deep knock-out dreamless sleep.

My fantasy is that one day I'll wake, it'll be say, 10.30am, and I'll do this enormous cartoon-ish yawn, stretch my arms above my head and declare, 'Ah, I slept like a log.'
Anna Kisby, from 'Your Stories'

Every day has its own rewards, but every day is difficult. I just want to lay there in the morning and have an extra 10 minutes' sleep, but I can't.
Interview with B, daughter 15 months

In the past two months, since she has been sleeping through the night, I sleep like a piece of wood and have hardly any dreams, which is really unusual because I used to have really vivid action dreams. Usually, I travel a lot in my dreams; in my country, we say that if you dream of travelling, you will miss out on

Photo: Cécile Chevalier

something. I have many dreams about losing teeth or meeting family members and I have arguments with them.

Interview with H, daughter 16 months

S-mothering

I've never been one for exercise. Getting all sweaty for no reason? No thanks. I'd rather have a cup of tea.

I've always tended towards the podgier end of the spectrum, but two kids later, my podge is turning into something else – it's taken on a life of its own.

Where there were once generous curves and the odd bulge, there are now pendulous, lumpy, tired-looking folds.

When I lean forwards, I can feel the weight of the skin on my face being pulled towards the ground.

The bags under my eyes will never be eliminated with a product from a tube – they're etched into my face, like someone's been at me with a knife.

The knife of countless, endless nights not sleeping.

YEARS
Of dragging myself to work, trying and failing to appear functional and normal.

Trying to carry on achieving, working, earning, talking, walking, breathing.

Mothering, it's smothering.

Something had to give in order to keep going through the mirk,

To keep going through the work.

Met with unsympathetic faces in meetings – expecting me to remember things! To speak in coherent sentences!

Who were these jokers, why did they not understand how not sleeping makes you feel like you're in quicksand?

Standing and breathing and walking are major achievements...

Come on guys, give me a hand! Don't stand and gawp and bitch and talk. Help me.

So, the quicksand didn't get me, you know. It didn't swallow me up.

Instead, slowly, things shifted.

You got the idea that night time is for sleeping – although the 5.00am wake-ups could do with a review.

We're so lucky to have you both – the pain of the early years drifts away into something far sweeter.

Life is better when you have a sleeper.

Megan Kendall

My day until now

It began before sunrise and will keep going. One day merges into the next, and so on it goes. Without enough sleep, I am often at the edge of reason, almost coherent and holding practicalities together.

This is true in mostly all my tasks, except for one job: Jasmine. She wakes me up in the morning with her sweet bubbling voice and a wonderful smile. That is in the morning, before sunrise. She wakes me every two hours with a small groan as she pokes her head above her cot railings, looking in the dark for me, her comforter, her mother.

Breastfeeding, laughing, crying; shower; 'The wheels on the bus go round and round'. 'Please bear with me sweet angel, I need to wash.' Toothbrush, hairbrush; tickle tickle; 'Let's put your socks on.' Promptly dropping everything to the sound of her screaming in the distance. Comfort on call! Parenting is a paradox. Displacement.

Caren Fisher, from 'Your Stories'

Co-sleeping

She's had such a bad stint of sleep – I've never been that tired before and I don't think anyone can comment on it until they've been that exhausted. We did co-sleep at the beginning, but it was uncomfortable. To be honest, it was him more than the baby. I felt pulled because I wanted to share the bed with him, and only him, because that's what I missed from before; but I also needed to be there for her. I think you constantly feel pulled.

I found the first six months of her life really difficult. I wouldn't go back to that if I was paid. I found it really, really tough. I didn't know what to expect and it's just so hard.

I'm close to my mum and I love her, but I've found her really irritating since I got pregnant. I don't know why. I feel bad because everyone seems to see their mothers in a really positive light.

She's good with my daughter. I did talk to her about feeling lonely, but that was when I found her most irritating. When you're trying to cope as best you can, trying to look after a baby, and you have a partner who's getting home from work and you're trying to be strong for them, I think you need your mum to step in and just look after you. She did it as well as she could, but not in the way that I needed. I should have told her, but I didn't know what was going on – I didn't know what I needed.

Interview with K, daughter 8 months

What do you mean she's in bed with you? My mother was appalled and sure we would crush her. It must be confusing, I mean, advice has changed so much since the 60s:

'Never take your baby into your bed – there is a great risk of suffocation!'
'Place your baby on their back to sleep.'
'Place your baby on their side to sleep.'
'Place your baby on their front to sleep.'

Ultimately, you just have to follow your instincts. It felt lovely having her in bed with us. Besides, it was the only way any of us could get any sleep. She just wouldn't settle in a Moses basket. The only downside was getting such terrible backache from staying in the same awkward position on my side, with my arm up over her head and under my pillow, so she could easily access the milkbar throughout the night.

My dreams have been so vivid since my daughter was born. For the first few weeks, I had a recurring nightmare about tripping up and dropping her down the stairs. These bloody steep Hanover stairs. I kept waking up in a complete panic, only to find her quietly lying next to me. Safe.

Kate Ballard

She sleeps well at night. She sleeps in bed with us – I think that helps her sleep and I think in the long term it's a good thing – obviously, I know it's not what a lot of people do, so it's been getting difficult as all our babies grow up to discuss those things,

Photo: Kerry Ghais

because everyone's doing things so differently and some people have very strong opinions about breastfeeding and sleeping. I find myself biting my tongue about a lot of things. Because you can't tell people what they should and shouldn't do. It's not your place, and every baby's different.

At the beginning, I thought I was never going to have any energy again. She didn't sleep much – she cried a lot; I was just too exhausted to enjoy it because it is draining; and I felt really guilty, thinking, 'I've been looking forward to having this baby for ages,' but I was just so tired. I'm actually preferring this bit by a long way.

She can interact, she can tell me what she wants; whereas in the beginning, I think she was quite frustrated and she would just scream, and I think she didn't want to be placid. And she smiles and she socialises. And she sleeps, so I can sleep; it's just a completely different world, it feels so different – waking up in a panic because she was

crying and not knowing what to do, not knowing how to fix it, and having so much advice, being so overwhelmed – it was not nice. At three or four months, it all started to change quite a lot, and it's gradually improved.

Interview with S, daughter 8 months

I sometimes wake, yearning to be able to turn from the side lying position I have held for many hours around my beautiful baby and just simply flip flat on to my back, legs outstretched, arms laid out beside my body, palms up. Oh, to then let go! Fully let go of my body weight and sink into the depths of the mattress! That would be complete bliss. I can't sleep; but if I don't, I won't get the rest I need to be a good mother tomorrow.

The more I feel the pressure to sleep, the more it recedes from my grasp. Desperation increases, tears release themselves in frustration.

Caren Fisher, from 'Your Stories'

I wondered what the secret was

I expected things to change when I became a mother. People had told me it was hard.

I knew I'd be tired. But then I wouldn't have to go to work, I thought, so I would be able to rest; I wouldn't have much to do, I thought, so it wouldn't matter if I was tired – compared to commuting 50 miles in the snow to a full-time job while heavily pregnant? This was going to be respite, lovely snuggly time with my baby.

I expected that my 'self' would be sidelined. I knew I would have to put my baby's needs before mine, knew I would want to do that. But I wouldn't be working, so I wouldn't have anything else to do. My partner would be with me in this project – he and I shared everything. We were tight; we thought the same way. We could do this, it would bring us closer together – everyone said that about having a child. You bond and then you're a family. My own family would help, too, and I'd have plenty of time to meet up with friends. I'd get babysitters and still go out.

Well, actually people can't prepare you, as all mothers know. Someone once said to me after I'd had a baby that in life there is a chasm with two groups of people on either side. One is parents, the other non-parents. The parents can see it. But the non-parents don't know it's there. Unfair to those without children perhaps, but it spoke to me at the time.

Tiredness permeates every aspect of your life. Life takes on a different colour when you're being woken up every hour for a feed and then can't go back to sleep because you've got a baby on your belly. Or when your baby is cluster feeding, all night. When you get about an hour's sleep some nights, two on others. Broken up into snippets of wipe-out sleep you drag yourself out of when the baby cries, because you know you have to.

The loneliness I wasn't prepared for – the long, long nights of being on my own. Standing next to a cot at 2.00am, holding a little hand, getting cramp, wondering how long it's been since they closed their eyes, how long before you can let go without waking them. It feels like hours. It may be only minutes – 10? 15? 20? But it's boring and wearing, standing there

stock still in the dark when you're exhausted. You never quite wait long enough, and your departure sets them off again, back to square one. More long minutes standing with only your bleak thoughts.

Because your thoughts are bleak when you're sleep-deprived. Small things became huge, insurmountable. The daytimes were a blur. I felt wobbly and sad all the time. I couldn't do anything because I couldn't just put down my son. My life was feeding or sitting uncomfortably while he slept on me, a cold cup of tea just out of reach. Tasks like the washing seemed mountainous. It took me weeks to work out how to put up the buggy; and during those weeks, I thought about my failure to master it all the time. Leaving the house took a huge amount of effort and headspace – I was usually doing it because he hadn't slept – walking helped him to get him off – he didn't sleep much during the day.

And my 'self'? Well, it didn't get sidelined. It disappeared. I became a feeder, a vessel. I never had any time to myself, I was permanently attached. I didn't choose attachment parenting – my baby did. I could put him down for a minute but he would wail.

'My third child just gets ignored, sadly,' a friend once told me. 'How do you ignore them?' I asked – I genuinely wanted to know. I wanted to ignore my baby, too, sometimes, but he would just scream at me until I picked him up. I could never stand it for long, and saved those moments for the most urgent and essential tasks, like going to the loo or putting a couple of pieces of bread and peanut butter in my mouth.

If I managed to have a shower, I put him in a seat in the bathroom and rushed through my ablutions while he screamed.
I never knew why he screamed. I remember sitting on the bed while he lay in the cot, crying. I was crying, too. I'd tried everything. I screamed back at him, 'I don't know what you want!' It didn't help.

My family dropped by. It was lovely to see them. They brought thoughtful presents and cake, and love. But, of course, then they went home. I didn't see much of my friends – most were working, so they weren't around in the daytime, and I was too tired – and busy feeding – in the evening. I never had people round for lunch because I couldn't put him down long enough to prepare any food. I simply didn't understand how other people managed to make food. I wondered what the secret was that I was missing.

I couldn't go out because he breastfed all night; I couldn't get the breast pump to work, and when I persevered, I managed to squeeze out enough for half a feed. In any case, I was too tired to socialise. I joined some baby groups, but everyone just seemed so smugly together, happy and relaxed, that I never felt comfortable. It felt wrong to tell them how hard I was finding it all – like I'd got the wrong script and they'd turn on me as a bad, unloving mother.

I didn't know what to say to people when I saw them. 'Yes, it's wonderful.' 'Oh, you know, a couple of hours.' 'He's so gorgeous.' But, inside, I felt so low, like I was clinging on.

I asked the health worker. I told her he fed all the time and screamed when he wasn't feeding, that I wasn't sleeping and I was finding it tough. She said that was normal, to just keep on doing what I was doing. 'It must be all right, he's a good weight and he looks healthy.' She wasn't interested in what it was doing to me.

My partner was completely absent. He didn't share in anything. It was partly because I was breastfeeding, partly because he didn't know what to do; a lot because he didn't feel it was his job. He didn't seem to feel a connection with his son, either. There was no desire to be part of the parenting. So when my son was colicky, I held him, rocked him, took him for walks for hours every afternoon while he screamed; and when my partner got home after work and I was desperate, I'd ask for just half an hour without the baby. He refused. He'd been at work all day – what had I been doing? He wanted to relax. With his computer. And his wine. At one point he told me I was lucky, I had a dishwasher. His mother had brought up him and his brother without such mod cons and you never caught her complaining. I wondered how I had married a man from the 50s without even realising it. Turned out he didn't think like me at all.

I asked a neighbour one day as I arrived back home after walking the streets with my baby in a sling, a little scrunched up face screaming at me, nose to nose. 'Does it get better?' 'No,' she said. 'It gets different.'

She was wrong. It did get better. I'm separated from my son's father now. I'm far, far happier. I love my son. I'm sure I don't need to say that, but it seems relevant. He is part of me, my little heart running around outside my body. We are great friends and we have a lot of joy in our lives. But I could never have contemplated doing it again. It's hard, they say. But you can never really know quite how hard until you're there in the darkness, alone with the screaming and your own exhausted sense of failure.

Anonymous

6. Me and my partner

Space, sleep and sex

Everyone says that their relationship with their other half changes when they have a child. It can raise tensions as sleep deprivation kicks in, it can interrupt intimacy – 'He feels kicked out of his own bed, not needed,' says Anna Kisby, as she talks about a night-time fight – and sometimes it can feel like the fun has gone out of a partnership. 'As for the drinking, bonking, decadent weekends, lying loving, all those random snogs, hugs – where did they go?' says Chloe Forfitt. Some even separate. But others are more casual. 'Obviously, there's been some tough times and stress, but having him hasn't totally changed our lives,' says U. And many find their partner steps up to the plate to share the experience of parenting, and they find a closeness in their new family unit. 'It's a good balance, the three of us,' says R.

I miss us
How is it that my partner and I spend more time in the same space together than we ever did, but I still miss him? We have a new intimacy and shared pride about our son, but no time for the old intimacy of life before our son. We've been through this huge experience together without time to digest it, muse on it, share it together. I miss our weekend mornings eating croissants and reading the papers… not that we spoke much then anyway – we just were, we had time. How exotic and delicious that time seems now. I have no idea when we will have it again.
From 'Your Stories'

She'll pick her up, play with her
My partner is very proactive. When she comes home from work, she'll pick her up, or change her nappy, or play with her. Originally we thought she would carry our child; but she lost a lot of weight, and we weren't sure if she was fertile. That's the great thing about being in a lesbian relationship – you can swap. I'm

making light of it, but obviously it was a big decision – we did think about it a lot.
Interview with M, daughter 9 weeks

He lives nearby
I'm not married. I have a boyfriend; we don't live together. The choice is not to live in the same place as my partner and it suits both of us, at the moment; and he's nearby. He comes to our house at weekends, so I can please myself most of the time because I've not got anybody else other than the baby to focus on. He's a good dad.
Interview with Q, son 4 months

It's a good balance
I've been with my husband for 11 years. We always wanted to have children, but we didn't want to rush it, as we met when we were really young. He's really happy with my daughter and really ecstatic about being a dad. It's a good balance, the three of us. He works from home on Friday mornings and then he has her in the afternoon. So he has some time to himself with

her and he really enjoys that, and it gives me a break. The thought of five days ahead – it's not so bad when it's four days, it's okay.

The baby drudgery and the being on your own – there's loads of things you can do to make it better, by going out and doing things. But you can't escape the fact that you are tied to a person all the time, and it's wearing when you're doing it 12 hours a day. I think the next 10 years are stretched out ahead of me, which feels like a long time. You do get to a point when you need a break, and having that extra time when I know he's going to be at home – psychologically, it makes it so much easier. He really likes it as he misses her when he's at work.
Interview with R, daughter 6 months

Testing times

I'm not married, I have a boyfriend. We've been together about two and a half years. The baby wasn't really planned, to be honest – not in a bad way. We were in Australia and I fell pregnant there, and I didn't find out till I was about 10 weeks. It was all a bit strange, really, as we'd just come back and we'd led a totally different lifestyle in Australia, and then I was pregnant. We decided to move down here as I'd signed up for a course at the uni which was only part-time, so I carried on and did that.

My relationship with my partner has been affected, as we're a bit snappy with each other sometimes, purely due to tiredness and probably my frustration. It's generally the days when I've been alone with him all day and not really spoken to anyone. He comes home, and I'm probably desperate to talk and have adult conversation, and he's tired from work and only half listening, and that frustrates me, I think; and we might snap at each other then. And not able to have those lie-ins at weekends and doing those nice things. Apart from that, we're still pretty similar and still have a lot of laughs. He's very relaxed, and I'm quite relaxed in general. Obviously, there's been some tough times and stress; but having him hasn't totally changed our lives.

We have a sense of family; but day to day, I don't think about it. We try and take him

Photo: Kerry Ghais

swimming every Sunday so my boyfriend gets to do some activity with him. Last Sunday, I didn't really feel like going in, so I just went and watched; it was really weird being on the outside and watch them be together. That was a moment of realisation, thinking, 'Oh, that's my family.' It made me feel really proud. I also remember in the hospital when I had him. I think when you get over the buzz when everyone goes home, and you're left alone – I think I drifted off for a couple of hours sleep when he was sleeping and woke up and looked over – and the realisation of, 'Oh that's mine.'
Interview with U, son 6 months

We fight. We fight over how to deal with E waking every three, two, one hour – leave her to settle, pick her up, feed her; is she really hungry, is she teething, is it just habit; do we break the habit, do we comfort, does N stay or go; who needs sleep more – me or him? We fight to be generous to each other: 'I'll take her,' 'No, no, you sleep – I'll take her.'

One night – it's probably 2.00am or 3.00am and we've already woken several times – I suggest he sleeps on the sofa because he has work in the morning. He doesn't like to do this, he says sleeping separately is 'a giving up on our love'. I like that he feels this, I call him 'a soppy old thing' – but sometimes needs must. I badger him. He storms off with a dramatic parting quip, 'See you in six months, then!' He feels kicked out of his own bed, not needed. The next day we laugh about this, giggle over his drama-queen flounce. We rarely fight in the daytime. In the daytime we do our healing.

Anna Kisby, from 'Your Stories'

I'd known my husband for some years but we hadn't been together long when I got pregnant. We got married a month before he was born. It got rid of the expectations. It felt like it couldn't be perfect, because we were rushing things. I couldn't be bothered to choose a proper dress, it just had to be one that fitted...

He has been a fantastic dad. It's tested us in terms of snappiness and tiredness, me wanting a break when he gets home from work. He's a borderline workaholic, he's used to being able to work all night and weekends if he wants. We have to establish boundaries over work and home life; we're getting there. He's very good at wanting to know if I'm having wobbles about things, or feeling cross or having doubts.

Interview with C, son 4 months

'You got what you wanted'

I thought I couldn't have a baby because I'd had chlamydia years ago, and the doctor had said I might have blocked tubes. I was in my early 20s. I felt I wasn't worthy, that I wouldn't have a normal family life. I split up with my long-term partner of nine years – we'd only tried on a few occasions and, because I'd not got pregnant, I was convinced I couldn't have kids. It was really silly looking back, I just wish I could have had an investigation of my tubes,

which takes about three minutes to do. You lie there, they put the stuff in and they can visualise on a screen.

I got an ovulation kit – it showed I didn't ovulate till day 17. I think that was my only problem, because I fell pregnant that month. I wasn't whooping with delight because I felt stunned and ill. I was already being sick the first day of my missed period. I was throwing up my porridge, and it was a dead giveaway.

I was sick every day for months. I had a horrible pregnancy with all day long sickness, not morning sickness. It was hyper-emesis. I was in hospital twice with a drip. You worry that the baby's going to be all right and you feel selfish for taking drugs, but I couldn't even keep water down.

When I got pregnant, my ex said, 'You've got what you wanted, now get on with it.' I felt I was here on my own – this is essentially my baby already in my mind. He took me to be seen in outpatients and was annoyed because we had to wait, and he missed the start of the rugby.

Interview with F, son 17 months

Scared to have sex

My sexuality is not a priority at the moment. It pops up into my mind that we don't have much of a sex life, but I think it's probably because I'm tired and because I'm devoting my energy to my daughter. I don't know whether I'd say I feel less sexual, but I don't feel at the moment that I particularly want to have sex a lot. It's on hold a little bit while I give my daughter my energy. I'm hopeful it will come back because it's a large part of being a woman and of a relationship, as well.

I think my partner's ok with it. It's been ok when we have, I think he's probably just happy to get it when he can – he's as tired as I am, too, as he gets woken up quite a lot. He understand that that's where my energy is at the moment. For a few months after the birth, I did have a little bit of fear around sex because I tore – I didn't have stitches, but I feared I could open up the wound, which I guess is probably quite common. It's gone now. I healed, and I've had sex, and I haven't

Photo: Kerry Ghais

reopened up. That was probably something that held me back a little while.
Interview with P, daughter 9 months

Being intimate to make a baby
It's odd, the difference when you're intimate with your partner, that's just for the sake of it; but when you're intimate to make a baby, it's so different. You're thinking, 'Is that it, am I pregnant?' Maybe we should do it again, like he's a performing monkey.
Interview with E, daughter 9 months

Where did all the random snogs go?
'When you're 30, shall we make a little one of us?' my boyfriend drunkenly whispered. 'Are you mental?' I replied.

Turning 31 four days ago, feeling more tired than I did at 30, but less tired than I did last week – hurrah! – I reflect upon the seven-week-old little one of us. I'm snatching half an hour as my little one has just gone to sleep.

My partner will be home in 30 minutes, and I want to tell him how much I appreciate him; how sorry I am that I seem to have changed beyond all recognition; that I have no attention for him, no kind words, no love left on a daily basis that will stretch to hold him too. We'll see how that goes.

In seven weeks, I have become a different person. When I walked through the door, home from hospital, I couldn't believe the flat was unchanged. There was still ice on the ground. In fact, how was it that people on our street appeared to be going about their daily business as usual?

I don't know what I expected. For them to form a chorus line and welcome me into my new life, with high kicks and a song, like in an old film? Or just to stare, wide-eyed, at this new miracle that had somehow made it into our lives, via my vagina? The insanity of that fact still grabs me at odd moments. I'm still being asked what the birth was like. I find myself saying, 'Oh yes, it was fine, all good.' Apart from the ring of fire. I'll never listen to Johnny Cash the same way again.

I feel incredibly lucky that I was able to have such a good birth. The postnatal bit, though – that's a different story. Is it a secret, a horror that shall remain unspoken until you've got the baby out? Obviously we couldn't tell you when you were pregnant. Why the hell not?! It's not like I could hold her in.

We all live in our disconnected social bubbles, where mothers occupy a separate realm, just as old people and teenagers have theirs. Now I crave community, not just companionship of other mothers with babies – though that is imperative – but mothers who have older children, teens who may be considering procreation, grandmothers who have the wisdom of age and do not necessarily have first grandchild syndrome. They just want to hold the baby. Oh, for someone to come round and hold the baby.

This is something I cannot criticise my partner for. He's very good at holding the baby. Just about everything else, though, I can have a good old whinge about. I had no idea our relationship would change so much. We are now like co-carers who live together. We discuss the needs of our little one and try to organise eating, sleeping, feeding, changing, dressing – fairly and without rattiness. As for the drinking, bonking, decadent weekends, lying loving, all those random snogs, hugs – where did they go? Will there ever be the

possibility that I can get enough energy back to be sexy, friendly... civil? Our new relationship with this being, who remains psychologically and emotionally part of me, and takes all my energy to sustain.

I know I must leave the house each day to retain my sanity, I know I must tend to her every need. I already feel guilty that I am not stimulating her enough, that I should be doing more.

The other day, I had a few cups of special Neals Yard postnatal tea my friend had sent me: lavender, St John's Wart and calendula. After a while, I called her to ask if she'd tried some of this brew, as I felt really good but a bit lethargic and E had been asleep for rather a long time...

'You're not supposed to drink it,' she shrieked down the phone, 'You're supposed to sit in it!' which I'd say is a waste as E and I had a lovely afternoon, giggling. I even got some housework done. I can now see why housewives in the past were addicted to valium.

Chloe Forfitt, from 'Your Stories'

He gets to sit on the train
I miss my old life; my partner doesn't so much because his life hasn't really changed that much. He's a very devoted father and he loves spending time with her; but he's doing a course, so he's out a lot at night still. He's doing his job. He goes to London, he gets to sit on the train.

Interview with G, daughter 14 months

7. Friends and family

Where does the support come from?

In one of our exercises, women write about a close relationship that has changed. Many choose to write about their partner, but often they have been surprised by a change in relationships with family or friends. 'Facebook taunted me with pictures of their other life, their proper life. I was conveniently cropped,' says Claire Jones-Hughes. 'I expected I'd make closer friendships with mums than I did,' says K. Many fare better. R says, 'I wouldn't want to always be hanging around with people with babies all the time, but it's nice to have those friends who understand where you're coming from.' And some learn something about themselves. 'I realise what a rubbish friend I was when they were pregnant – I feel ashamed of my behaviour,' says I.

The way women are treated in the first few months I think is horrendous. I was told so much stuff: get used to having no sleep – you're not going to have any for 18 years. At the time I took it really seriously and I was quite upset. I was quite anaemic as well, so I had really low energy levels, and people just say really insensitive things. I think there should be more support for women in the first few weeks and months; that would help build the foundations for them for the next few years. You need someone to be there for you.
Interview with S, daughter 8 months

A long way from home
My mum and dad live up in the north of England; I moved down here; my mum can't come down whenever I need her – I go up there now regularly, about every two months when I've got annual leave. They'd really like me to move up there – they don't put pressure on me directly, but I feel it. She's trying to be practical, she wants me to go so I can have more support. I'd love to be near them and I don't want them to be missing out on what's probably going to be their only grandchild – I'm

an only child. I feel a bit emotional about that. I moved away years ago and I've never gone back properly.

You do crave time with your family and being close to them. It's something to look forward to when we go up – he enjoys being physical with granddad. The trouble is, I've been in my house so long. I know you can make your home anywhere, but this has been good to me because it was a housing association and I can't afford a property on my own like this. I'd only be able to afford a one bedroom flat.
Interview with F, son 17 months

My family lives in Europe. We talk a lot on Skype. We're going to see them at the New Year. My father is a sensitive man, in touch with other people's feelings. He was actually afraid to pick me up when I was a baby. I said to him, when we visit I'd like him to pick her up – we want her to have contact with men.

We do have male friends and my partner has a brother, but he's a bit of a globetrotter. He went a few days after she was born. But he fell in love with her. He said, 'I never knew what the fuss about babies was, but then I held her.'

He had no intention of coming back at Christmas, but now he is coming back. There's also my partner's dad, but he doesn't live locally.
Interview with M, daughter 9 weeks

Maybe not the in-laws
I could never have done this without support. While I don't let people in easily, you have to. It's their wellbeing and your wellbeing at stake. Maybe not the in-laws. They want to visit every month. It's the night times. She's their first grandchild, though. I have to have words with myself – I know they want to share in it. My husband's been a great gatekeeper, though, so they don't come down more often. Both of them smoke as well, and he's been very firm with them. He's said they can smoke in the garden and hold her an hour later but not any sooner. It must have been incredibly difficult for him to say. His mum always arrives with a suitcase full of stuff for her. He has to tell them we don't need all that. I know it's because they love her, though.
Interview with O, daughter 2 months

You gain some, you lose some
Perhaps not the most devastating thing when you become a mother, but definitely one of the saddest, is that while you're adjusting to life being pregnant or with a small baby, you look behind your shoulder and see that some friends haven't followed down your path.

I resigned myself to the fact I was the one who had radically changed my life – I should make the effort.

We continued to play phone tag for weeks, it was like trying to catch a fly with your bare hands. After hours of over-analysis, I was left bemused, flicking through photo albums of old times. Wondering if I had done something wrong. Why hasn't she called? Facebook taunted me with pictures of their other life, their proper life. I was conveniently cropped.
Claire Jones-Hughes, from 'Your Stories'

I've not really got lots of friends. I had two friends when I was at work before I had the little one – they went a bit distant, were really childish.

I go to lots of baby groups. I like my baby groups – it gets me out of the house. I've become very good with my own company – just sitting on the floor with the little one, crawling around, playing with toys – that's usually how I spend any free time when I'm not out.

My fiancé is my friend. I think if a relationship can go through having a baby, then it can go through anything. It is the most testing time in anybody's relationship. She was kind of planned – let's see how things go if I don't use contraception... 'Oh my God, I'm pregnant.' No, it wasn't that quick, to be honest – it took about a year.

He's a really good bloke – everybody says you can tell his top priority is making his family happy. He says before he had the little one that his life didn't really have purpose. And I can see that, because now our purpose is raising her, making her happy.

My dad sees us once a week on Wednesdays – we go to Asda, food shopping. He sees her for about 15-20 minutes; then we leave, go to Asda and separate.

It's not proper time, but he's a man at the end of the day – he's not interested in, 'Oh she winked,' and that sort of thing. I don't see my brothers and sisters a lot, but when we do it's good quality time with lots of conversations, catching up.
Interview with J, daughter 7 months

The main adaption I've found is not being around adults all day; not getting up and going to work; spending a lot of time on my own in the flat. Even if I go out and do something in the day, it will only be for an hour and a half, and spending all day with a baby is probably the main thing you're not quite prepared for. Sometimes that's hard, and sometimes I love it, and sometimes I don't even think about it. I think if I've spent too long on my own, say I've been in all day in the flat, I do get a bit frustrated. In the summer I went out for walks with him even to buy a paper. I've normally got something to do every day, even if it's just getting a bit of shopping. I try to do some mum and baby groups, as well, so I've got things on in the week.

Photo: Kerry Ghais

I've been lucky actually, as I did pregnancy yoga and met three lovely girls, and we all had our babies around the same time and we're in contact still. We all do mum and baby yoga, and sometimes we bump into each other at baby boogie and things like that. We were all quite shy at first, probably because you almost feel a forced friendship – just because you're all pregnant doesn't mean you'll get on. But we've all clicked naturally and they're all girls I would have been friends with even if we weren't pregnant, so that's been lovely. That has been a big help as none of my old friends have babies yet – I'm the first one.

I lived in London for eight years before I came here and I'm from Kent originally. I've got friends mostly in London. They have been good and they've tried to visit quite a lot, and I try and go up a fair bit, as well. I've done a bit of travelling with him. I was quite conscious of that – that I didn't want to feel like, just because I have a baby, that I couldn't do anything. So from the start I was quite active, which has been good as it's given me the confidence to know if I have to get on a train, I'll just get on a train.

One of my good friends had a baby six months older than him and she's been great – she was so independent and buzzing about everywhere with the baby, and it showed me in a way that I can do that. She's in Kent, so I don't see enough of her as I'd like to. I was quite conscious that I'd like to meet some mums here, because even if my good friends had children they're not down here.

Interview with U, son 6 months

I found the loneliness really hard. I expected I'd make closer friendships with mums than I did; I felt like my friends from before I had a baby were off leading exciting lives, full of sleep and fun and careers, and I was…
Interview with K, daughter 8 months

My family are reasonably far away, but they do come down and visit quite a lot. We're the first ones to have a baby among our close friends. But I have met some good friends at various other things. It's a good mixture. I wouldn't want to always be hanging around with people with babies all the time, but it's nice to have those friends who understand where you're coming from.
    My old friends are very supportive and really involved, too. They love her and want to look after her, and they're like aunties and uncles to her – it's brilliant.
Interview with R, daughter 6 months

When my partner and I moved here, we left quite a lot of our friends behind. My partner is like my best friend. One of my friends back home was jealous that I was pregnant. She accosted me because I'd fallen pregnant so easily; we have a rather strange relationship now. Another one of my friends smoked throughout her pregnancy and she's still smoking now. I thought she'd stop – we had a bit of a spat about it. I said I thought she was being selfish. What you put into your own body is fine, but when it impacts on another person… it's still a bone of contention. Some of us have matured, but others have entered into pregnancy without having let go of our previous lives.
Interview with E, daughter 9 months

All the friends that I had when I lived in London are still doing the same sort of thing, and I live in Brighton with a baby. I find having things in common really difficult, so those friendships have come to an end, more or less. I'm sad about that. I can't just be running up to London to go out for the night. Our lifestyles are just so different – even though I can see where they're

coming from, everyday conversation is very difficult.
    None of my siblings have any kids and yet I still feel close to them – they have a vested interest in her.
Interview with G, daughter 14 months

I think the way I see friendships and people I spend time with has changed. Because time is something I value more now, especially if I'm going to be spending time with people while my daughter is with someone else, I want it to be someone whose company I really enjoy, I want it to be someone I really like.
Interview with S, daughter 8 months

Most of my friends have children. I realise what a rubbish friend I was when they were pregnant – I feel ashamed of my behaviour. I was quite humbled by how they were to me – their interest and sheer delight in my pregnancy.
Interview with I, daughter 4 months

Childless friends don't understand at all. They suggested going out for cocktails for my birthday – I just want to sleep.
From 'Your Stories'

I've found myself thinking about other friends who have children, and how I hadn't really appreciated what they had before I had a baby – thinking they must all feel like this about their kids, and they've just been really normal. I just think, 'Am I really neurotic or something?'
    My best friend's got two children but I never appreciated the intensity that they have. When their first baby was born, I remember thinking, 'Oh, they're really obsessive parents, they can't let go' – like having conversations with them and they're not listening to you – and now you appreciate that. I think I was a terrible friend because I just didn't appreciate what they were going through – looking after this little person who's suddenly the most important thing in your life.
Interview with P, daughter 9 months

8. My own mother

Whether to follow her, or forge a different path

Motherhood inevitably makes women think about their own mother. It takes many back to their own childhood. 'I was hard work, very hyperactive and just didn't listen to my mum … I'm picturing my baby being the same, and thinking about how hard it must have been for my mum and how hard it might be for me,' says S.

Many are in awe of their mother's achievements. 'She's amazing, she worked full time and we didn't have any money but she gave us so much,' says U. Others feel that they want to do everything differently. They can be annoyed by their mothers' attentions – cue more guilt. And Ali Norrell rounds off this chapter with a salute to the maternal line.

A thank you to mothers
Thank you to the warm mothers
who make sure babies are fed
and children are hugged,
you are the first to teach us what it is to be
loved

Thank you to the solitary mothers
who need their own space
and never have time to play,
you show us how to be our own mothers
with our own minds

Thank you to the wild mothers
who rage and cackle, fire in belly,
you teach us the instability
and flux of life,
allowing us to love all things
with fierce passion,
creating and destroying with joyous abandon

Thank you mothers
for your ever giving breast,
your strong steady arms,
hard working hands

You gave me your heart
so I can feel,
you gave me your eyes
so I can see

I have your tears
so I can heal your scars,
I have your bones
to carry on the story of this universe
Ione Milner-Gulland

Advice
My family are bonkers
My family are mad
Why did you give me the advice
That you have?
Anonymous, writing session

Respect
Mum – how do you do it? How did you do it? Four kids, five jobs and a man who never helped; no gadgets, quick fixes, a culture that cared about appearances more than you. The opposite image of women cooing softness, oozing love, your love was more practical, more

hard; your energy has got me to where I am today – fulfilled and happy in a good space. I wish you would have had time to be tender, gentle and loving. I remember so well those precious moments when you played with my hair. Your strength and tenacity are a credit to you. It makes me wonder if I can be like that.
Julie Canavan, from 'Your Stories'

Hopefully, my baby would think I'm very loving and caring, and quite relaxed. I'm not really a big worrier. My mum's the least dramatic person ever, and I think that's helped. When we were growing up, even big things she really played down. So anything that happens with him, I've not been worried and just dealt with it. The midwife that came round when he was three days old said, 'Your baby's really relaxed,' and my partner and I both seem relaxed, and that's probably why.

My mum brought me and my brother up on her own, and I'd like to think we're both pretty well-rounded people. My brother's absolutely lovely. When we were teenagers, we were very different: I was very sociable, and he was studious and quite shy. When we were older, we both moved to London at a similar time and got really close. He was there at the hospital for the birth. He's not got kids.

My mum's still on her own. My mum and dad were together when my brother was born, and then they split up. I've never grown up with my dad. She had a partner for a while when I was a teenager, but that didn't work out. She's amazing, she worked full time and we didn't have any money, but she gave us so much. I think she showed me you don't have to have a lot of money to have a good upbringing.

We haven't got much money – my partner's on a low wage – but it's never worried me. I know people stress about it, and my friends think they can only have children once they're on a certain salary level, but you don't have to. I know once they're older they'll cost most, but they don't have to. We always had clothes from a charity shop, and you can get lovely stuff.

My mum's got the perfect grandma relationship – she comes and has fun with him and loves being around him. She respects the

way I'm bringing him up and asks me things like, 'How do you do this?' and, 'How do you want this done?' If I ask her, 'How should I do this, mum?' or, 'Do you think he needs a coat on?' she's there if I need her, but she doesn't interfere. She wasn't interfering with my pregnancy at all – not like, 'Oh, I've done it,' which I know some mums can be. She's very balanced. Whenever I've spoken to her about him, she tells me it's just a phase and that helped prepare me, I think.
Interview with U, son 6 months

At the moment, I would describe our parenting as accidental. My memories of childhood are of being outside a lot, or doing baking or creative things. I have visions of doing that with her, but she might be an IT geek. Although it would be difficult, because I'm not a home-y person.
Interview with I, daughter 4 months

My relationship with my mum has completely changed. I keep telling her, 'I'm sorry I ever told you I hated you' as a teenager. At the beginning, I was really hormonal, really emotional, and I was speaking about it to her and apologising to her. I feel like I'm more on my mum's level now, like we're a part of something together.

My younger sister was off school and my mum was feeling really guilty and saying, 'You've got a child now, imagine if she'd been off school for three weeks how you'd feel,' and trying to relate to me on that level, which is quite different. I like it, but at the same time I feel like my mum's quite different to me in how she sees the world; so although we relate to each other a lot better now, we're still very different as people.

I feel like I'm parenting in a similar way, but that I still want to do things slightly differently, do things my way. I understand why things were the way they were when I was growing up now. I come from quite a large family, and everything was very hectic and chaotic. But everyone looked after each other, and I understand that support network now and why it was so important. Now I'm living in Brighton with my partner and no family around, so I can

Photo: Kerry Ghais

see the difference when you are surrounded by supportive people.

But, in terms of thinking children should be children and letting them learn in their own time, rather than enforcing some sort of routine or structure from very early on – my parents were never like that, and I don't think I'd want to be like that, either. I did go through a phase of thinking maybe we should be teaching her to sleep and that sort of thing, but I didn't really follow it.

I worry about her telling me she hates me as a teenager. At the beginning, I was terrified of everything, and thinking about what a difficult child and teenager I was. I was hard work, very hyperactive and just didn't listen to my mum. I used to hide behind clothes rails in shops as a toddler. I'm picturing her being the same, and thinking about how hard it must have been for my mum and how hard it might be for me. That was scary at the beginning when I was really hormonal and exhausted, but now I see it as more of a positive thing.

Interview with S, daughter 8 months

I'd like to have another baby quite soon. I had a small age gap with my sisters. We're still close now. I had three sisters, but the youngest died when she was very little. My mum was nearly always gentle and calm, so you knew if she was upset or angry, you'd really done something wrong.

My dad wasn't so consistent: sometimes we'd all be punished until one of us told the truth – he lost his patience too easily. I do love my dad, but he's a product of his own upbringing, which had more fear in it. I have more respect for my mum.

My mother was with us for the birth. She was quietly supportive: the only time I remember her speaking was when I had to push, which I found very difficult, because I was exhausted after two days of contractions and not being able to eat very much because it made me feel sick. Afterwards, I felt bad, thinking, 'Why didn't I try to eat more?' but she told me to stop because everything had gone well. She said it in a very gentle way. And then I felt good about the birth.

Interview with L, son 7 months

37

I'm much happier – I hated living at home; I didn't like being the person that does everything at my dad's house; I had wanted to move out since I was 13. I know it sounds like a childish reason, but I had nothing to myself. I had my stuff in my room: if it was clothes, my sister would have them; CDs – my brother would have them; DVDs – my dad would be like, 'Can I watch that?'... then, 'Look, he's scratched it.' Then, randomly in the middle of the night, I'd have my little sister or brother in front of my telly, and I'd be like, 'Get out.' No privacy. When I got with my fiancé, about six months in, we moved in together.

My dad is quite a big man – he's had heart problems, he smokes, he's unhealthy; he was rushed into hospital once – one of my earliest memories is of him with things stuck to his chest. If something happened to him, I could not step up to the plate and have my brother and sister come – it's not fair on my daughter. I know that sounds selfish, but I can't share myself out that much. My older sister couldn't. She just got married, she's in a little cocoon and I can understand that. I could see them going into care, or going with my aunties or uncles.

Interview with J, daughter 7 months

A different path

There's so much information out there, so many decisions you have to make, sometimes you just have to go with your gut. I left home when I was 11 because I didn't agree with the way my mum lived her life. I've got quite a few brothers and sisters. Where we grew up was quite socially deprived – a council estate – abuse is acceptable behind closed doors.

It was quite a big journey going from being an independent, career-minded woman to falling pregnant, seeing my parents as people rather than parents. Just questioning a lot of things.

Where I'm from, it's the norm to have kids quite young. My brother's got three; he had the first when he was 20. He got in touch with me when I was pregnant; he's such a relaxed parent, playful – he reminded me of some of the good things about when we were growing

up. We kind of broke off into splinter groups and parented ourselves.

I went to see my dad when I was pregnant. He was more interested in his new partner and I ended up flipping out at them. She just sat there, chewing gum, and hardly said anything. I was upset because I'd had barely any contact with my dad for ten years. My brothers and sisters have all got children, so I suppose it's old hat to him. It's quite broken as well with my mum, quite fragmented. I don't know how I'd feel about it if she just turned up. It's quite a small town we're from, so she has to put on an act, keep up appearances.

If I went up, it would be to see my gran. She was the person who took me in. She was very independent and she did a lot to facilitate me being independent. She gave me little household chores to make me responsible. It showed me how a family worked, as in how the home was run. There were certain things you needed to compromise on. She gave me normality and stability. She was pushy as well, with education. It was a balance between that and my mum who was too relaxed.

I found I was going to extremes. Showering my daughter with so much attention, everything had to be educational and developmental, but now I've taken a step back and just let her be herself. I've spoken to my partner a lot recently about how we should be there to facilitate her, take a child-led approach – not Baby Einstein and all that, pushing them to adulthood. It doesn't suit everyone, like my sister-in-law, who's a Gina Ford woman through and through.

Interview with E, daughter 9 months

I'm doing it completely differently to my mother. My relationship with her at times can be strained. And it's partly to do with my upbringing. My mum is quite a selfish person and quite self-centred – I've always felt that through my life. She always loved me, she always showed me love, but she didn't give me the attention that I craved, so that's what I want to do for my baby, I want to be there for her. I want her to know she's the most important thing in my life. That's one of the things I didn't feel growing up. I had a very bad relationship with my stepfather; I always felt that she took his side and it was them against me a little bit.

I want to do everything I can for my daughter. I feel that it's really important that I do the best for her, show her that attention. It's just little things, like my mum never asked what homework I had and my friends would say, 'Oh my mum's nagging me to do this homework,' and I thought, 'My mum never even asks me what homework I've got.' I felt that she wasn't really taking an interest. So I want to take an interest, without being overbearing.

Since I've had my daughter, my relationship with my mum is changing a little bit because I'm more appreciative of what she went through when I was a baby. She must have felt these similar emotions. I never appreciated that she nurtured me and looked after me when I was a baby, I never really thought about it. And actually she did have a tough time for a while when I was young, because her relationship with my dad was quite bad so she was a single parent for a little while. Now I really appreciate what she did for me because the thought of raising a child on your own – I've got absolute admiration for anyone who does it because it's quite hard work.

I don't want it to sound like we've got a really bad relationship, because we've got an ok relationship. It's better if we see each other for short periods, though – I think it's quite common in a mother/daughter relationship, anyway. My mum never really praised me. Even now, she doesn't necessarily praise me to her face, but I talk to other family members and they'll say, 'Your mum's so proud of you,' but she never tells me that. She's very good at almost showing off to other people about me but she never acts it to me, which is a real issue. I want to tell my daughter when she gets older how proud of her I am, what a great human being she hopefully turns out to be. I want her to be happy, just happy in herself more than anything, confident in who she is and happy with her life.

Interview with P, daughter 9 months

It's been helpful having him because it's a topic of conversation with my mum. It doesn't have to be about anything more fraught. Unless she's being critical about something I'm doing. I think the biggest thing is, she thinks I should leave him crying more: 'It's ok if they're crying because they learn to entertain themselves. I just left you, so what's the problem?'

We're going up to see her and she said her friend would babysit so we can all go out for her birthday. I said evenings were a bit tricky, because he was often quite grizzly and wanted to feed a lot. She said, 'If you're not ready, that's absolutely fine.' I felt angry – it's not that I wasn't ready, it's that he couldn't take a bottle yet and he'd be crying. She said her friend would be all right with a crying baby, she didn't understand that I wouldn't be happy if he was crying. It felt like a really different approach. If he was unhappy, I'd want to pick him up and comfort him; she can't see that.

Obviously, I don't know what my mum was like with me as a baby. She protected us and kept us safe; there's lots of things about parenting us I'd take from her, but I definitely feel the baby stuff is different. My dad wasn't very good with babies – she was on her own with us a lot, although she had a maternity nurse to come and stay.

I think she's quite impressed I'm doing everything. It made me feel quite weird that there was someone else who'd looked after me for the first months. It's hard talking about it now.

Interview with C, son 4 months

My relationship with my mother has changed dramatically. I thought it would become closer before I had a baby. I've discovered a lot about her since having a baby and I've discovered the way she is can have a strong bearing on me; and I can see that affects my child, as well. I don't feel as close as I did. It's not exactly friction but there's a bit of a stand-off between us...

My mother still lives in Australia – we used to talk on the phone a lot – I think I used to depend on her for advice a lot more. I've stepped away from her. She worries a lot and she puts that worry on to me. With your children, you worry enough about them as it is without somebody saying, 'Oh you should go to the doctor' or, 'You shouldn't do that to your child.'

I think that's a lot to do with motherhood. My approach to bringing up my daughter is a bit different – not that I think I had a bad upbringing, but I definitely have different views. I have a much more earthy approach to things from having a home birth. I didn't want any drugs unless I had to. I wasn't one of those mums who said, 'Bring on the epidural.' The decisions that you make as a parent just evolve from there.

Interview with G, daughter 14 months

Walking down the street, holding my hand sometimes: 'Yes, you must – because of the cars.' My parents never used the words 'I love you', and here is Eleanor declaring love for everything around her. Just utterly fabulous and beautiful to hear.

Rebecca Tonge, from 'Your Stories'

I don't cry at the TV, unless I see my family or relationships mirrored. If there's something about someone's dad dying, I want to cry – my dad's really unhealthy. I had a dream once that he died, and I woke up crying. I worry about him because I haven't really got my mum any more. She decided about five years ago to go and live with a man she met on the internet. So my dad's the only parent I've got left.

She left my brothers and sisters, as well. My little sister was five. My dad had to quit his job and look after them. I had to step up to the plate, too, sorting out dinner times, sorting out breakfast. From when my little sister was born, my mum was pretty lousy, she didn't want the place to be tidy, she didn't bother. It was me changing the nappies. I haven't had much contact with her, just a few emails. I had an email when the little one was born saying 'Good luck,' but it's just what I didn't want – to be honest, I didn't want her to contact me. I wanted to show her I could be a better mum than she could.

Interview with J, daughter 7 months

Photo: Kerry Ghais

It's always in my mind that I don't want to be like my parents. I want to do everything completely opposite to the way they did. I remember not playing with them at all. We were always taught we mustn't do this, mustn't do that. There wasn't actually anything we were allowed to do. It was like everything was forbidden. The relationship is like not having parents at all. There are no arguments, there's nothing.

It's like I'm not part of their life any more. As soon as I left their home, I was forgotten completely. I saw them at my grandfather's funeral, and before that it was two and a half years. They've never seen my child. They never asked how she is or sent a birthday card. On the other hand, I get 200 times more love from my partner's parents – they treat me like their own.

Interview with H, daughter 16 months

Don't Spoil Her!
As if my love is poison
that she drinks from my breast

As if listening to her
gives her the idea
that she deserves to be heard

And looking at her
could make her feel that she is innately
beautiful

Best not
delve into
such dangerous things
Ione Milner-Gulland

Walking the maternal line
Not so long ago, my seven-year-old daughter and I invited the girls from her class to a gathering at our home with their mamas. She attends a small independent school, so we all fell comfortably into place around our kitchen table for tea, cake and chat. By coincidence, our little party happened to coincide with both International Women's Day and Mother's Day in the UK; and as the afternoon wore on and the teapot passed, emptied and refilled, we found ourselves deep in conversation about mothering.

Discussing our daughters, and what we hoped we would pass on to them in terms of traditions and positive, life-affirming beliefs, we found ourselves sharing our stories of what we hoped our daughters would inherit from our own mothers and their mothers before them – and what they might discard. We were all walking an ancestral line and adhering to programming passed from mother to mother over many generations; sifting and sorting each element and deciding what to pass down.

This woman, our mother, created us and carried us. She birthed us, gave us life, so it is inevitable that we feel her in the deepest recesses of our DNA. Sometimes we look at her and see a mirror image of ourselves. Those with children will often exclaim in mock horror following a fraught exchange with offspring, 'Oh my goodness, I sounded exactly like my mother!' The mother/daughter relationship, and all its associated push and pull, is as old as eternity. We moan, we complain, we admire, we wonder how we will ever live up to her standards, we wonder why she never pursued her goals or why she pursued them too hard; and through it all, we are inextricably bound together in each other's dramas.

I recently came across a photograph of me with my mother and maternal grandmother. I am around a year old in my mother's arms. It's a crisp sunny day, we are standing outside in the garden of my childhood home, and both women are smiling proudly. The family resemblance between we three is startling. When I gazed on this familiar photograph, I felt a pang of regret that my own daughters were not present in the line-up.

My eldest bears an uncanny resemblance to her great-grandmother, both physically and in temperament. When she is asleep, I sometimes fancy that I see her face morph into that of my grandmother Eleanor, for whom my daughter was given the middle name of Elen. My younger daughter – a mirror image of myself in this picture – died at the age of four months. I wonder if she too would prove to have inherited her grandmother's steely determination, rebelliousness and sharp intelligence. I suspect not. Even in her short time with us, she displayed the even temper and calmness I associate with my own mother.

The photograph reminds me that, although my grandmother did not enjoy a particularly close relationship with her daughter during her younger years, becoming a grandmother softened her and took the edge off what we suspect was debilitating depression that plagued her for much of her life. A mother and housewife during the 50s, my grandmother came from a modest background and was not afforded the opportunities that I had. I imagine that she occasionally found her existence as a younger woman cloying, repetitive and downright dull – feelings that most mothers of any generation can associate with, but when you live with depression can become all-consuming. Mental health was not talked about then, and so she struggled on, occasionally taking out her regret and dissatisfaction on her family.

My mother, in contrast, took to life as a wife and mother, and sometime office worker, with consummate ease. She was ever-present in the lives of my sister and me, and never gave us cause to wonder whether she would rather have been elsewhere, doing something else with her life. Her happiness and contentment at being at home with her children shone through, to the extent that it caused me to feel a degree of guilt once I became a mother because I did not see this in myself.

Thanks to my mother, I have never found the words 'I love you' to stick in my throat. I also learned, by example, to be kind and empathic to those in need. I remember one Christmas watching her place cash into an envelope for strangers. She worked in a public service office and an elderly couple had come in to pay a bill. When my mother informed them that in actual fact they did not owe money, but that they were due a small refund, their palpable relief at having an extra £20 available just before Christmas moved her to tears. She clandestinely looked up their address on the office computer system, placed some cash in a Christmas card and signed it 'From a well-wisher' before posting it off to them. I have never forgotten my admiration at this act, and have tried to emulate my mother's giving nature at all times in my life. Almost greater than the pleasure of helping others in this way is that of witnessing the same behaviour artlessly displayed by my own daughter. Somebody recently referred to her as 'The kindest person they had ever met' and I could have burst with pride.

My mother is, unsurprisingly, a fantastic grandmother, always ready to play and with seemingly endless reserves of patience. All our children adore her, and whenever I have found it necessary to spend more than a couple of hours apart from any of them, Nanna is drafted in as an excellent 'stunt double'.

I recall how crushed I felt when my mother kindly, but very emphatically, refused my invitation to be present at the births of her grandchildren. She was adamant that this was not her place, that she would be 'intruding' on a private moment between my husband and me. Notwithstanding the fact that I worked as a birth doula for a decade, I would jump at the chance to attend the births of any of my grandchildren, should I be fortunate enough to be invited. Even if I am not, I will doubtless find a way of inviting myself.

I have every intention of interfering in my daughter's life as much as possible, in direct contrast with my mother's consistent efforts to tread lightly and only when invited. Given the strength of my personality, I admire her wisdom, as always, in judiciously keeping to the background. If she had my propensity for diving headfirst into things, it would be a marvel if we were actually to get on at all. Instead, my mother's insistence on not giving unsolicited advice has meant that on the occasions when she elects to do so, I sit up and listen. Over the years, I have become eager to set in place a whole host of traditions for all our children – my daughter, in particular – based partly on what my mother did, and partly on what she didn't.

At the end of it all, we can only do what comes naturally to us and try our best to incorporate the best of our ancestors. For what is motherhood but a glorious patchwork quilt: each square contributed by ourselves, our own mothers, grandmothers and those before them, the unfinished article passed down via our daughters to future generations? We have all made mistakes and embroidered over them; the finished effect is one of mismatched colour, fun, warmth, and practicality all sewn together with love.

To my knowledge, my mother did not live with depression, but it has not been a stranger to me. After my youngest daughter died, it hit me like the proverbial ten-ton truck; but after the initial intensity subsided, I began to see that it had hovered persistently in the background for most of my life – I just hadn't called it out. My grandmother's constant assertions to me that I must use my intelligence, get out there and make my mark, helped me to push through some difficult times. Sometimes it served to remind me that I can place other titles proudly alongside 'mother', that I am still a valid person outside this, the most gratifying and the most thankless of roles.

Ali Norrell

9. Close to you

The all-consuming love of a mother

The loved-up chapter. The women in our groups don't just talk about the tough times – they celebrate their children, their bond and their lives with them. How to explain it? 'The intensity of love and joy is overwhelming,' says Rebecca Tonge. One mother talks about how she would love her child even if she were a serial killer. Some find their love, at times, hard to bear. 'Your mortality terrifies me,' writes Ione Milner-Gulland in 'Scared'.

So insidious, the slow separation of your child from you. As they separate, you get parts of yourself back – it is painful and bittersweet.
From 'Your Stories'

Never
Never has a job been so mundane, yet so monumental,
so gutsy, yet so sentimental
so all day, so all night
so stroke my hair, hold me tight.
Never has love been so unconditional and understanding,
so giving and so undemanding.
Never have I had so much to do, yet done so little;
never have I appreciated each day as a time of growth, a time of change.
Each moment is an opportunity for wonder, for discovery;
never have I delighted at the near sight of eyes and a smile
as we pause and connect, skin to skin, for a while.
Anna Kisby

Consumed
My, how the time just passes as I potter about with you. Sitting on the sofa, you curled up next to me, head on my lap, scribbling in my journal; asking me to draw a funny man; looking into your eyes and stroking your head.

The intensity of love and joy is overwhelming – I am utterly consumed by you, and I don't care if we are going to be late. I just want this moment with you.

And it's like this every day. Changing, developing, growing, understanding. This little person before me. Strong, defiant, cheeky and so, so clever. Your new sideways glances, the jumps when I catch you doing something you know you shouldn't. Your boundless energy and gentle nature.

Blonde curls, fairy wings dancing, jumping up and down on the bed. What does mummy say? 'No!' – huge grin.

And the speed with which you grow and change. All these babies. Lovely as they are, they are not you. They could never be you. I wouldn't want anyone but you.

And I want to bring you into the group and say to all these new mums, 'Look! Look at what your baby will become,' – my love and pride really know no bounds.
Rebecca Tonge, from 'Your Stories'

I was just talking to my partner about how one day she's going to leave home, and leave us – it's just so awful. It's crazy because she's nine months old, and I'm just like, 'Oh, now how awful is that going to be, I'm going to be devastated...'

She sleeps well – she just wakes up a lot, so I feed her three, maybe four, times in the night. It's really hard, but there are those moments in the middle of the night when I'm feeding her and I'm like, 'That's my baby.' And I'm really tired, but I'll look down and I'm cuddling her while I'm feeding her, and it keeps me going...

I have moments when my emotions are heightened, when I think about my baby and the love for her – you can't believe how much you can love another human being at times. It's almost like your heart could explode. I just want to hug her really tight, which I guess I haven't experienced before in quite the same way – obviously, I have love for my partner, but it's quite different – it's intense to the point that, if I think about it, I could just burst into tears like, 'Oh my God'; it's completely overwhelming, it's like nothing I've ever experienced.

Interview with P, daughter 9 months

Bonding for me was immediate. I catch glimpses of both of us in the mirror, and a lot of the time he looks like me when I was a baby, but then certain expressions I look at and think, 'Gosh, that's my dad,' and that's really strange.

Interview with Q, son 4 months

To become a mum is to complete why you were born, fulfil the purpose of your being. That's what it means to me. I know the purpose of my life now. I always knew I was going to become a mother. If I hadn't had my own, I would adopt or foster, because I think it is natural for a woman to guide someone into life. To give what we have inside, because after a while I think everyone has too much and you need new people to give it to. When I took her to the medical centre the first time after she was born and I left home alone with her, she was four and a half weeks old. I couldn't wait to get to people to show her off. I felt really proud and that's when I realised I'm really her mum, this is where it all starts.

Interview with H, daughter 16 months

All I can think of is him, my beautiful boy. The sweetest, purest, most delectable love. I can't believe we made him, this cheerful, smiley, funny boy. He gets obsessed by certain things: bins – he wants to stop at every bin, to put whatever bit of rubbish he's just found in it. His smile, his laugh, his chatter.

Ellen Stewart, from 'Your Stories'

Sometimes I want to pinch myself that they are real – this man with the slant brown eyes who cares for me, this beautiful baby with his eyebrows and a smile that stops passers-by. When I look at her, I am overwhelmed by how perfectly herself she is. As Sylvia Plath wrote of one of her babies, 'A clean slate, with your own face on.' That's E for me, and I wonder and wonder at it, and feel joyful.

Anna Kisby, from 'Your Stories'

I'm probably a bit more sensitive than before, but I'm a laid-back and calm character, so maybe that's why I've got a laid-back baby. I think you get the baby that suits you. He's joyful, and he wakes up and smiles. I don't have any crying at night. He wakes up to feed and goes back to sleep again.

Interview with Q, son 4 months

Watching something I've made grow into a complete person far outweighs the joy I remember experiencing when I first grew some tomatoes from seed. That's nothing at all compared to growing a baby from scratch.

Megan Kendall, from 'Your Stories'

I'm not a touchy-feely type person. I was a bit worried before I had her that I wouldn't be able to cuddle her. I found out that my parents never picked me up as a newborn, which was worrying me. She was born and it was a revelation, it was the complete opposite. It's impossible not to stroke her, look at her. I feel closer to my friends with children now and closer to their children.

Interview with M, daughter 9 weeks

The first time I went out, she was about six weeks old – quite young to be with a

Photo: Kerry Ghais

babysitter, but we really wanted to see a film. I was on the bus and I was like, 'Something's missing.' She is part of me, and I think about something I heard the other day about being a mum – she doesn't belong to me, I belong to her. That is definitely how I feel, everything I am I give to her, everything I can do – I would do anything for her. I'm getting emotional again. It is a different kind of love from your partner to your baby. You love your partner, but I love her unconditionally – she could be some serial killer when she grows up, but I'd still love her.

Interview with J, daughter 7 months

I couldn't accept he was mine

It took me a few weeks to accept he was my baby. There was part of me that expected the day to come to an end and him not be there, like when you look after a relative or friend's baby and they get taken home. That feeling has stopped now, I can't pinpoint when it did.

It is hard work and unexpected sometimes, but so rewarding. I read somewhere that a baby's first smile is usually at the point when you're dropping with exhaustion after the first few weeks – it's like nature's way of encouraging you.

Interview with L, son 7 months

Living in the moment

One of the best things about being a mum is being forced to be in the moment. Sometimes she will just not let me cook or do anything. She's like, 'You have to be here with me.' I do, and it's lovely. I make her smile when she's grizzly, I hope I always have room for that. There was one time we were on the motorway and she was really upset – I was torn between just getting home and sorting it out there and pulling over… I thought, 'I'm going to pull over,' I pulled over to give her a cuddle. We must have sat there for about an hour. It was lovely. I could carry on, guilt-free, with the journey.

Even though she started crying again, I thought, 'I've cuddled you for an hour so you know I'm here, but we've just got to get home.'

Interview with A, daughter 6 months

Anything for a fart joke

She's practising her latest skill: blowing raspberries. She woke in the night and I picked her up, hoping she would slumber. She was wide awake, clambering up my body and desperately trying to wake me up. She lifted my nightdress and put her lips to my belly to practise her raspberry-blowing. Keeping very still, I tried not to encourage her or respond… until a large sound issued forth from her lips. She burst out laughing, and so did, in turn, my husband and I. She repeated the action three times. Just like her dad, she never misses the chance to perform a fart joke.

Caren Fisher, from 'Your Stories'

Tethered

The best and worst bits of being a mother are one and the same for me. It's having the ultimate responsibility: nowhere to hide, nowhere to run to; no calling in sick; no emigrating, no emptying the bank account and doing a runner; no 'Not tonight, dear – I've got a headache'; no scrapping what you've done and starting again from scratch; no excuses – you are held in place, you are tethered to the earth.

Anna Kisby, from 'Your Stories'

I was at a baby group, and I went to the toilet and someone was keeping an eye on my daughter. I came back in and looked at all these babies on the floor and I thought, 'That one's MINE.' Or if she's next to me in bed, I just melt. Or when she's with my partner. It's the observing moments. Sometimes you're just so busy, feeding, changing the nappy, trying to get somewhere, that you feel like it's just a job and a job title – 'Mum'. But at other times you think, 'I'm part of this group now.' It's a whole unknown world you've come into. Someone recently said I was such a fantastic mum, which was really sweet. People don't turn round and tell other mums that they're doing a good job very often. We don't do it enough.

Interview with E, daughter 9 months

The protection instinct

I get more emotional since I've become a mum. Seeing people losing children – that really turns me out and I'm crying my eyes out for them. Seeing cruelty to children. It really reminds me of who I am and what the purpose of me with my child is – to protect her in any situation – or it may be just the love I feel makes me really protective, being afraid of losing her.

I'm the same in some ways since she came, but in many things not. My partner would say I'm completely changed. He would say I'm completely concentrated on her, which might be true. But for me, she's the number one and he's the number two. It might not be the same for him – I don't know, because I can't feel what he feels. I don't feel much different, but I know that I am responsible for someone now; and it comes from deep inside, so I don't have to remind myself. It's in my unconscious mind, because I don't think about it – it comes naturally, an instinct.

If I have to speak English to her when we're out, she gets upset with me. If he speaks English, that's ok – it's only me who's not allowed to speak to her in English. I think she can't recognise me when I mix up the languages. The way she treats me then it's, 'Go away, you're not my mummy.' She understands both languages completely.

Interview with H, daughter 16 months

Right from the first night, I was aware that my body had suddenly become totally alert to my new baby's presence. Although I was exhausted, I was hyper-aware of her tiny noises and movements, and I couldn't bring my body to sleep. When she was suddenly sick in the cot and appeared to be choking on vomited milk, immobile and lying on her back, I leapt in the air and rushed over to her, panicking. My partner continued snoring on the sofa bed. A pulse of adrenaline went through my body. I realised this is how it was going to be from now on: I would sleep like a guard dog with one eye

open for the rest of my life, and he would always be able to switch off. I felt the weight of huge responsibility on my shoulders.
Anonymous

Too fast

Before I even have the chance to discern how to feel about your growing, changing form and frame, I am besieged by images of first rolls, crawls and teeth, and the same identikit pleased and satisfied reactions from parents across the land.

I enter the world of social media under misapprehensions of solidarity; and leave full of unfavourable comparisons, cut adrift and thoroughly unsure. The smiling, proud moments of others leave no space for my own ambivalence about such 'milestone' moments. And those cards. Those cards should come with a health warning. Particularly the one emblazoned with the words, 'I slept through the night for the first time!' I don't need to see that. To whom does such an achievement belong?

Surely I am wrong to feel so mixed up about you growing up, and to meet your precious moments with such a regrettable response? But you are moving too quickly for me, and I don't know how to process these moments in a way that I can remember them. I don't know how to record them in a way to properly capture their essence. I try the cards but you stare quizzically at the camera phone, your eyes boring knowing holes through my inadequacy.

I feel panic rising; the fear that I am letting you down and doing a disservice to your history is palpable. For, without a trail of public announcements and accompanying photographs, does your infanthood really exist at all? Will your future self be wounded by a lack of collective memory about your younger years?

I mourn time's passing before we've even begun. A year's maternity leave – 'luxury' though it may be – is sliced up with vaccination schedules, weaning on to solids, crawling, walking. The presupposed itinerary stretches in front of us and we act out each phase as it dawns. I field an endless list of enquiries about whether you have rolled over yet, our chosen style of weaning, and – surely the worst –

whether you are yet in 'a routine'. I become more reluctant than ever to share these details with the world. They are not for others to own.
Anonymous

We have a lot of giggles together. He's a very happy baby. Even if I'm feeling tired or if I'm not feeling that excitable myself, I do try and do big expressions and make everything lots of fun for him. That has now started to really show, as he giggles a lot and that's quite rewarding...

They grow so quickly, and sometimes I think, 'Did I really appreciate when he was tiny?' I look at him and think, 'You're not a tiny baby any more,' – and I miss that. I think the early days, you're so tired and it's always about feeding, and you don't get time to appreciate them. Whereas now, I'm feeding him every few hours, so I've got more time to appreciate him and play with him.

I get really sad when I have to pack away clothes that don't fit him any more that I've loved him in. I look forward to having another one; but I don't want to rush it as I want to fully focus on him, having those stages of crawling and walking, and give him totally my time first. I was looking at him the other day thinking, 'Imagine if he's an older brother,' but I don't want him to have that just yet.
Interview with U, son 6 months

Only I will do

I feel it's hard talking about your parenting choices because people are so delicate about it. I don't want to be judgmental about it, but I am. I want it to be just me that looks after him – I'm thinking about not going back to work after my maternity leave.
Interview with C, son 4 months

I love to play with her. Sometimes she's asleep, and I'm wishing she wasn't because I want to play. I sense sometimes she wants me to put her down because she wants to look around and have time for herself, but I love holding her.

Normally she's very calm, but this week she had her shots. As a teacher, I think it's very important she has her injections. People who choose not to have to rely on everyone else having their children immunised. It was horrible going, though. She was fast asleep and she woke up as I put her down on the bed in the surgery. Then the nurse arrived with the needle and jabbed her, and she screamed. I felt really guilty. Next time, I'll make sure she's awake, because I don't want her to be surprised like that in her sleep.

One day, she was really scratchy. A friend of mine came to visit and was holding her trying to bounce her, but she was really crying. I took her, comforted her and she fell asleep. I thought, 'It's me, I've got this power, nobody else has got it.'

That's when it hit home it was me who was her mum, who could do this. There was nothing my friend could do.

Interview with M, daughter 9 weeks

A couple of weeks ago, we had a friend round. My daughter started crying when my friend and my husband held her; but as soon as I held her, she looked at me and stopped. It was as if she knew she was safe with me. It's quite a responsibility, as well. I'm the only one who can stop her crying, I have to be here. It is a conversation I have with my mum quite often because I am a control freak, so I have to learn to let go. I want her to be securely attached, not overly attached.

Interview with O, daughter 2 months

Wings
Born to the sound of seagulls, your
first word is caw,
caw. Caw-caw.

I pour
the whole slippery mackerel
of my nipple
down your noisy gullet
and you take it,

your elsewhere eyes resolute
on flight.

How much you don't belong to me.
I curve my palm between

your blades
where, through skin, wings
begin to break.

Anna Kisby

An independent boy
From what I've seen of other mothers, he's quite independent, he's not needed to be cuddled in or protected all the time. It sounds quite strange for a baby. Even from when we first brought him home, he was quite happy to go on his play mat and play on his own. That's probably made it easier for me, especially in the early days. Now he's moving a bit more, I can't leave him as long the way I used to. I used to be able to go out, make a cup of tea, make lunch, and I'd know he'd still be on his play mat and he'd still be fine; but now he's wriggling around.

Interview with U, son 6 months

Scared
I find it painful to look you in the eyes
sometimes.
I've tried to hide away from my love for you
Keep the distance there
Because your mortality terrifies me
I'm so scared of how fragile your tiny body is
I'm not brave enough to hold the responsibility
of the possibility that you may die.
So I try to keep you at arm's length if possible
But you keep coming to me.
Nestling in closer. Pressing your small soft face
on to my skin.
You look at me like I'm the best thing you've
ever seen
The only thing you really need.
You know that one day I'll die and you accept
that
Too young to be foolish enough to try to cheat
death.
You know underneath there's no need to hold the
belief that worrying about the future could do
anything to make it suit you.
You just love with all your heart. Live with all
your body.
I'm hoping to be as wise as you, one day.

Ione Milner-Gulland

10. Who am I?

Disappeared in the service of another

The changes in women's sense of identity is a common theme in Mothers Uncovered sessions. Many redefine themselves ('It's a process of mourning your older self and adjustment,' says K), but often feel that they have become an attachment for their baby, which can be both positive and negative. 'I remember going to the supermarket on my own... for about half an hour, and that was really weird as I noticed the absence,' says V. Or they feel that they themselves have disappeared in the service of another. Many celebrate their redefinition as 'mother' and can feel more emotionally aware. 'I am different, it feels like I'm stoned on love,' says M.

There's me, and then there's the other me who's looking after the child.
From 'Your Stories'

If I'd known
If I'd known what it would be like, I wouldn't have agreed.
I'm changed forever.
I will never be the same.
Parts of me have gone.
Sometimes, I mourn this.
I'm treading water every day.
I know endurance as never before.
I stretch out my arm, my mind, try to find those lost parts.
They return in tantalising glimpses, but they cannot be reached.
The little being demanded all that I could give and more.
No room for solitude, peaceful contemplation, dreaming about what I might do or be.

If I'd known what it would be like, I wouldn't have agreed.
I'm changed forever.
I will never be the same.
Parts of me have gone.

Sometimes, I celebrate this.
I run a marathon every day.
I know endurance as never before.
I see the world through another's experiences, opportunities and dreams.
I feel more fear, love and hope than I ever thought possible.
If I'd known what it would be like, I wouldn't have agreed.
But how could I not have known him, cherished him, protected him?
I'm changed forever but he's part of me, of us.
I'll teach him to change the world in his own way.
We'll start together, and learn from each other.
Then, as he splashes and glides across the water,
away from me, chasing his own hopes and dreams,
I'll search for those lost parts of me.
Who knows what I'll find, what I might already have become?

If I'd known what it would be like, I wouldn't have agreed.
I'm glad I didn't know.
Jenny Birchall

Mother – the similarity with 'smother' – the daft desire to crush your children's impulses, their individuality, their desire to be different and escape; to embrace them to the point of reabsorption. Motherhood is a process of long slow loss, a pulling away – opening up, letting go, and slowly drawing yourself back into something resembling a human; gathering in your empty belly, your breasts, your battered hopes, your fractured dreams, your vaguely recalled self, your heart – what's left of your heart, after you've sliced it up and wrapped it carefully in tin foil, and popped it in their lunch box next to the breadsticks and the homemade banana bread and the grapes cut lengthways, just in case.

KO, free-writing session

Me, a mother
I can't believe what a huge experience it is – there don't seem to be words to describe it. I look at mothers so differently now; I used to, like everyone else, ignore them, just women with pushchairs. But now I have such a huge respect for them.

Interview with K, daughter 8 months

I lived quite a particular kind of life beforehand. I don't compare the two lives. You have to accept this is how things are. I realise how lucky I am to have maternity leave and be able to do things with her, like taking her swimming for the first time… a lot of my life has been socialising and being out.

'Mother' feels like a more strict word that 'mum'. 'Mum' feels like my mum – it's hard to think of her saying that. I would like to be a mum to her, but you have to be a mother in the more abstract sense. I don't feel like I'm 'mum' – it's a label I'm putting on myself for her, I wouldn't give myself that name.

Interview with I, daughter 4 months

We stayed in the hospital three nights while we were working on breastfeeding. Coming home, there wasn't one thing, but you're very aware they're with you all the time, in a good way. It's like, 'Oh, I'm a mum,' and it feels weird saying it at first. I remember going to the supermarket

on my own, while my husband looked after him for about half an hour, and that was really weird as I noticed the absence.

Interview with V, son 8 months

I wouldn't be without him, they become your life, really. You can't go back to thinking of the time you didn't have them. I feel like, socially, I've achieved more now. I always used to be a bit bitter, like I couldn't go into the 'mummies club' – I felt excluded. I enjoy taking him to the groups. There's a bit of camaraderie…

When my mum or dad calls me 'mum', it brings it home to me. The recognition when you're doing forms, you write 'mother' for the first time. It doesn't really sink in when you've just given birth. Mother. Me. How did that happen?

Interview with F, son 17 months

I don't think I've had a pivotal moment yet when I'm aware of myself as a mother. There was a moment when I was pregnant in the NCT class when the teacher asked the mums to go on one side and the dads on the other, and I thought, 'Where are the mums? Oh, you mean me.' I think I've still continued to have that, when people say, 'I'll pass you back to mummy,' about my child. I feel like I'm going along with it. It would be better if I could feel the nicer sides of it, too – I tend to go to the darker side.

Interview with C, son 4 months

Where did I go?
You exist less when you're a mother. Nobody asks you how you are, and if you do dare to say, 'I'm not that great,' people look at you as if to say, 'What do you mean?… you have a baby.' I've become more self-reliant in looking after my emotions. If I try and rely on somebody else, I get a bit resentful because they don't see it so they can't help.

Interview with A, daughter 6 months

Stuck in a culinary rut
Never-ending cooking and cleaning, and it will be the same for the next ten years. There are 365 days in a year, so that's 3,650 days. That

equals more than 9,000 meals to cook, plan, shop and clean for. I'm already stuck in a culinary rut – how can I manage another 8,999 inspired ideas? And it needs to be nutritious and tasty and edible.

Plastic pots run rife in our kitchen – they randomly disappear, which drives me insane. Their existence drives my partner insane. Eleanor's table manners will drive my mother insane, which will drive me insane. I want to switch off from it all.
Rebecca Tonge, from 'Your Stories'

Motherhood
Harassed with tenderness
and stressed love
gentle caring
guilt or strength
Anonymous, writing session

Mourning the old life
All my peers have this great social life, they're on their career paths, they've got such uncomplicated lives. I had a long process of mourning who I was, my old life. Especially as it wasn't a planned pregnancy. We moved from London to Brighton, we were living in a shared house. It's not like we got married, then we bought a house, we had our nice jobs, now we're ready for a child.

I'd go to groups every day, but I felt like everyone puts on this happy front. I felt like everyone else was coping really well and loved it, that it was only me who struggled to get out of the house. I did meet people I could relate to, but I didn't feel close to them, because you don't know them, do you – relationships don't form that way, it takes time to build up.

It came to a head when she was about three or four months, and I just broke down – I thought I'd have made better friends by now. I have no old friends and I have no new friends to replace them. When she was six months, things turned a corner. I wasn't getting any more sleep, but everything felt calmer, like the storm had cleared. I felt before it was just the process of feeding and sleeping, no enjoyment. I look back, and it feels like such a dark time in my life, to be honest. Now she's nearly nine

Photo:Kerry Ghais

months, I have made stronger friends. With babies, when you're in it, you can't see – it's new, you can't imagine it being any different than it is at that time. You have no idea what it's like until you have a baby. I try and explain to my friends but I don't know the words to say why it's hard.

We have both said it's easier now, we enjoy her now. I've always loved her. We've always had a bond because I never wanted to be away from her from when she was born. It wasn't postnatal depression, it was my situation – I was just so lonely I felt like no one understood, that my partner didn't understand what I was going through because he was at work. It's a process of mourning your older self and adjustment. I feel now so much stronger for having been through it. There were things I used to be scared of and I feel like nothing is as scary as motherhood, nothing will scare me like this has scared me. So I feel like I could do anything now, I honestly do. It's given me a lot of strength. I'm getting there with confidence, it's building.

It's the most painful thing to become a mother, the process of childbirth. It's the most amazing experience, and it's the most tiring experience – it's just like all the extremes rolled into one. No one can be as tired as a new mum, as overwhelmed, as frightened. I found the responsibility terrifying. In those first six months, I'd look in the mirror and think, 'I don't know who I am any more,' – I didn't recognise myself. I find it annoying when

people say things like, 'Oh, she's a natural, she's taken to it so well,' about motherhood – not about me, no one's said that about me. I just think, 'Are they mad? Have they not realised what has happened, have they not realised how much their life has changed?'
Interview with K, daughter 8 months

I'd always said, 'I'm never having children.' Then later, when I was growing up, I said, 'Ok, I'm going to adopt. But I'm going to adopt a child the day before its 18th birthday, throw him a party and then kick him out.' I don't know what changed my mind. It's just one day I woke up and thought, 'I'm ready now, I want a kid now.' Before, I'd look at children and think, 'I could look after children, I could do the aunt thing – brilliant – buy them the noisy toy, give them sweets.' I never thought I could do it before.
Interview with B, daughter 15 months

Now I know what it is to have someone dependent on me. Very occasionally, I go somewhere without my little boy and I get a glimpse of my former life. I cross the street without waiting for the green man, pause to gaze in shop windows and sit on the top deck of a bus.
Ellen Stewart, from 'Your Stories'

Ambition
I want to have a poo in peace
It shouldn't be a dream
But small voices calling through the door
Make me want to scream
I want to have a poo in peace
Oh how I long for it
But calls of 'Mum' from down the hall
Sure make it hard to shit!
Sam Johnson

New focus, new emotion
I don't feel I'm the same person since I became a mum. I've not essentially changed, but you focus on things differently. Before it was just about me, although I didn't want it to be. I did want to have a child, I suppose you can be more selfish and you don't realise how

precious your time is. You get used to that over the years; and because I was into my thirties when I had my son, I was used to my own company. I think I'm more fulfilled, it sounds a bit clichéd, but I feel more whole. I've achieved more now.

I like the concept of being a mum, and that's what I craved for years. It's not what I expected – it's really hard work. The whole 24/7 thing, that you can't ever be off-duty. I know you go off to sleep and you're not thinking about them every minute of the day. When you're at work, though, you've always got to consider them. I can rarely go out in the evening at the moment. I can, but it's a bit of an art form getting it organised. You'll only go out if you think it's really worth it. You have to become more organised, much more aware of every ten minutes. Your timekeeping is much more important when you've got a child.
Interview with F, son 17 months

My emotions are all over the place. During pregnancy, I was studying, and the way I was using my mind was completely different to how it is now. I've gone through a huge change, from a role where I was theorising all the time and writing, to something very active and physical, and nurturing. I've had to keep stopping myself from thinking too much. When I was studying, I was thinking about going into teaching, but now I'm thinking I'd rather save some of that nurturing side of me for her.
Interview with S, daughter 8 months

My emotions were fairly extreme before I was pregnant. Like around my period, I would get really moody. I've felt, a few times, quite emotional. Obviously, just after he was born I was – I wouldn't say depressed, but I felt kind of tearful and things would easily make me well up. I think, in a way, it's almost kind of stabilised me in a monthly kind of a way; but I can, partly due to sleep as well, feel irritable in the day or feel real joy and have a lovely time with him. It's nothing in particular, just a lovely day in the park, in the sunshine, or something like that.
Interview with V, son 8 months

I don't feel like the same person at all. The turning point was my birthday. I thought I wanted to go out for a drink and celebrate with my mates, but we couldn't find a babysitter. Well, I didn't really want to find a babysitter, I couldn't be bothered with it all. I was really happy just to sit in, have a takeaway, spend the day with my little one and my fiancée, chilling out and having fun as a family, instead of my old life going out. As soon as I found out I was pregnant, I stopped drinking, just settled down and grew up. Very different.

I've become really emotional. If she does something new, I just want to cry because I'm so happy. I got new earrings that make a noise if I shake my head. She laughed, I kept doing it and she copied me. It was like, 'Oh my God, you just did that.' I nearly cried when her first tooth came out. Anything new she does, I'm just holding back the tears.
Interview with J, daughter 7 months

I'm more emotional. It's interesting, because there's nothing particularly drastic hormonally going on. Every day I check in with my emotions and think, 'How am I actually feeling?' At the end of the day, I try to give the emotion a place and a colour, and think how bad is it on a scale of one to 10. Trying to name it and place it sort of 'right-sizes' it. I shut my eyes – this is normally when I'm giving my baby her end-of-the-day feed – and if it's anxiety, I'll think, 'Is it really anxiety?' When you start to do that, you become more objective; then I don't feel so overwhelmed by it.

Before I had a daughter, my emotions, while they mattered, didn't make a huge difference to my day – getting on buses or whatever – but now the emotions make a big difference. My anxiety will make me agoraphobic if I let it, my fears really will overwhelm me if I let them. When my partner broke his arm so he couldn't help, I felt proud because I managed to cope with things without falling apart completely. It's always a choice, always an option. You don't know until you're confronted with things.
Interview with A, daughter 6 months

I've always been fairly emotional, but I guess my emotions are more directed now. They seem to concern my baby more than anything. She's never not in my mind, so it's really hard to separate what I feel about other things. It's almost like there's not enough room for emotional reactions to external things. Because I feel that all my feeling is going in to her.

Emotionally, you're in a different space during pregnancy – it's a period of quite high excitement and anticipation. It's hard for me to think before that time, but I'm probably more emotionally aware now.
Interview with P, daughter 9 months

I think each day is different. But some days feel so mindless and relentless, it's almost soul-destroying. You would never particularly want to give space or voice to these feelings, however, because not only are you so lucky and grateful to have a child – particularly if you waited as long as I did before having one – but also it would be an insult to yourself, your child, and anyone else with or without a child, to start feeling hard done by.

However, unless perhaps you throw yourself wholeheartedly into all things 'mother and baby' and really consume yourself in that, then there remains a struggle, or tension, between being a mother and all that that involves (and a lot of it does amount to cleaning and wiping and changing and washing!), and being the you that you have always been and all that that might mean on any given day.
Saskia Neary, from 'Your Stories'

When told to consider 'anger' in relation to motherhood, I wrote, 'Where is it gone?' or 'Is there any?' something like that – well, it came back with a vengeance. My second period came this weekend and, my God, I could have killed him – he broke the double buggy, and his slowness and the mess of the place. I could really have killed someone, it makes you realise what women have to live with, what I have lived with all these years – once a month feeling like my whole life is wrong, wrong job, relationships, friends, and then it passes – these last two years have been a wonderful

Photo: Kerry Ghais

thirties. I enjoyed the pregnancy, and I made a conscious effort not to be too worried about it and just let it happen, without being too uptight. Obviously, the very early bit I was a bit more worried and didn't count on it happening for quite a while, certainly not till the first scan to make sure everything was alright. After that, I relaxed a bit more.

I don't think I've lost anything. I'm not at all concerned about the things that I can't do now. I haven't had hurdles or obstacles as he sleeps really well, which I think is a major benefit for me. If you're sleep-deprived, that affects absolutely everything you do. So I consider myself very fortunate in that respect

I feel like the same person. I don't feel I've lost who I am at all. That I've gained is probably more the case. I've always had a positive body image and I've accepted the way I am, it's how I was made. When I was pregnant, I just had a big bump and it went. I'm only 3lb heavier than before I had him and I've only got stretch marks on my hips, two stretch marks, so I'm incredibly lucky.

Interview with Q, son 4 months

Stoned on love

It's funny, because I said I wasn't a touchy-feely person, but actually when I went to visit work I hugged most of my colleagues. I am different, it feels like I'm stoned on love....

When you are expecting, a lot of people try to put a downer on it, saying there'll be lots of things you won't be able to do for years. There's a part of your life you're saying goodbye to. People don't dwell enough on the positives, which can make you downhearted. You're pregnant, thinking, 'What have I done. Is this my life? Am I signing off my life?'

People should notice the nice things more, even though there's up and downs every day. But in every day, there is always a little something that is good.

Interview with M, daughter 9 weeks

rest from that rollercoaster – I've had some anger, but largely been walking round like a la-la brain wondering why people get so stressed with each other. I am alone with these feelings and the emotion rises again. I am tired, pulled in so many directions. I sit in this room wanting to cry, wanting to sob and roll into a ball and nurse myself – all the nursing, loving and stroking of my babes – do I do it enough? Is there enough of me to go round?

Anonymous, from 'Your Stories'

I feel lucky

I've waited a long time to be a mummy. I lost a couple of babies at different times, so he's very much wanted. He's all natural. I'm in my late

Cartography for mothers

Shared with my fellow mothers uncovered around our first Mother's Day:
This is a peculiar road we've taken; trod by so

many before and alongside us, yet so often mysterious and lonely.

It's been mapped out by those further down it for us to study and plan, and is scrutinised and scoped out in so many forums.

Yet still we must divine and intuit our way, and be surprised by challenges and rewards at every turn, both inside and out of us.

This is an unforgiving journey that is at once liberating and alienating, where we always feel grateful and frightened in equal measure.

However our present challenges are fatiguing or invigorating us, as we go into the Mother's Day weekend, let's allow ourselves to feel great gratitude and pride.

Let's forgive ourselves for our fears, and any falls, crashes or stalls.

Let's give thanks to ourselves for navigating this landscape each day; shaping another person's world and the centre of our own.

Let's recognise the realisation that there is only ever one direction to go in, and our little ones reveal it to us every day.
Claire Robinson

The vessel
I am a vessel
A sea of silence
I open to let your feelings in

Your frustrated, angry, toddler feelings
filling up my being

It's uncomfortable, a tight jumble
It's too much for your little belly
your hands balled into fists

I take it all
under the water
making waves,
I rock them
quelling the storm
gently, gently
the surface is still once more.

But underneath,
down
deep down
on the sea floor

that tightness stays in me

It piles up like rocks
jabbing at my heart
slowing my feet
it hurts
kept in until I'm alone
or bursting out when I let slip

Torpedoes of anger
Hurricanes of sadness

I'm sorry I'm like this
I'm trying my best
Ione Milner-Gulland

A lonely place
So, I felt like I was the only one having all these problems. Because you don't see other mums when you've just given birth, you're just in your house with these problems. I felt like I was on another planet, a zombie. I was so tired. I remember it was summer when she was born and I really didn't want to be stuck indoors, I really hated that. Everyone said just rest, but I wanted to get on with my life. I wanted to get on as normal, I wanted to go for walks in the sunshine with my baby, but I felt like I was in a rush to get over that bit. I felt totally unconnected with the world around me.

I felt really horrible, I didn't have any time to put on make-up, I hated the clothes I was wearing – I just didn't feel like me in the slightest any more. I felt like I'd been taken over by this baby. Not that it was her fault, but I felt powerless. I felt at times that I wished I'd never had her, which is a horrible thing to feel. I spoke to my partner about it, and he said the same thing.
Interview with K, daughter 8 months

With motherhood, you're constantly analysing. There's always something new to worry about. There are days when it's just you with the baby, which can be quite hard. I live in Hove and sometimes it feels there's only one walk you can do, along the seafront. I grew up near a forest, where there were lots of walks.
Interview with I, daughter 4 months

Early motherhood was a deeply isolating experience for me. At 27, I was a relatively young mother for my social groups – none of my friends had babies yet, and ten years later many still don't. The traditional gender divide between my partner and I became all too apparent as soon as we became parents. I saw him continuing to live much as he had before, while I felt fundamentally changed – and although I enjoyed a much more rewarding closeness with our son, I was also restricted on a completely different level to him. He was mostly physically absent due to working shifts, and when he was around he left the responsibility for childcare to me. We did not have what I had imagined a family life would be like – it was as if it were just me and the baby, with my son's father as a lodger who sometimes cooked meals and contributed money.

I lived on the outskirts of town, and my maternity pay combined with his meagre salary didn't extend as far as money for bus fares most days. I remember doing a lot of walking, carrying my son in a sling, and taking advantage of the times he fell asleep to sit down for a hot chocolate in a café. On one of these occasions, I had only just got my drink when my baby woke up and started crying. I caught the eye of another mother of a young baby in the café, hoping for some recognition of the struggle I was going through. When she gave me only a blank, unsympathetic stare, I felt devastated and alone.

But we make do with what we have. I remember the weekly asylum of the breastfeeding drop-in that I was fortunate enough to discover while I was still pregnant, tipped off by a friend who was having her second baby. I was undeterred by the 45-minute walk and steep uphill trek with the pushchair. Sitting in a circle with other mothers and frequently knocked over cups of tea, I was able to see a hole in the fabric of my sleep-deprived isolation, and find common ground in the challenges and high points of early motherhood.

Although the breastfeed drop-in was a lifesaver for me, the conversations didn't go as deep as I needed them to. Attending the Mothers Uncovered groups when my son was 10 months old was eye-opening: for the first time, there were mothers like me admitting that sometimes it was tough and sometimes they weren't feeling the love. The refreshing honesty and support of that course inspired me to go on to run groups myself when my son was older.

As mothers, particularly in the early months and years, we need communities of mothers and women who support each other, and share our burdens. As a single mother for most of my son's life, I've had to be resourceful. My own supporters have been books, friends, and mothers who are truth-tellers: mothers who can admit the difficulties of being a mother, as well as the joys.

Being a mother in a society where mothering isn't recognised, celebrated and supported the way it should be means we often have to find and create the networks we need to sustain and hold ourselves. But this process can be a catalyst for creativity and new possibilities as we break out of our isolation and find that we aren't, after all, alone.

Morgan Nichols

11. Coping – or not

The days when you lose control

Postnatal depression is the end of a road that many women travel down. Most do not go all the way; but nearly all new mothers have times when they felt they have lost control and cannot cope. An anonymous woman describes 'a full year of feeling deeply sad, choked and wanting to cry a lot of the time'. B says: 'My partner would come in; I'd hand her to him, rush off to the bathroom, sit there on the floor bawling my eyes out.' Another shares a shocking tale of domestic violence. G explains the depths that can accompany sleep deprivation: 'I would never ever harm my child, but I have more of an understanding as to why someone would.' And O rounds off the chapter with a dose of the nightmare colic.

Tell me,
What's the difference
Between madness and sanity?
A nightmare and reality?
What is that fabric that cloaks us
When nobody woke us?
The fabric that keeps all the bits of the self
Neatly nested, together, creating health

If I could weave that fabric
I'd sell it, and buy my own tropical island
With the fortune I'd make
Megan Kendall

The moments of joy never came

I don't use his name – I find it hard to connect the name that we chose with him. I don't know if it's because of the name, or because of a bigger issue of bonding with him. I don't necessarily feel he's my child, I feel like I would about any child in my care. I call him 'poppet', or 'chicken', or 'little moo' or something. I call him by his full name if I have to; it feels a little odd if people shorten his name.

When he was born, I just said, 'He's really purple.' I really felt like I was in a performance and everyone was watching me. That felt like the start of being watched to see how you're mothering. I was in hospital for three days, exhausted; but the pressure to say something meaningful to my baby in front of a room full of doctors and nurses was quite noticeable.

Some people, especially in baby magazines, talk about how wonderful the moment is when you hold your baby for the first time – it made everything worthwhile and everything else melted away – but a lot of others feel, 'Who is this stranger? I'm just tired and need a break.' I knew that, but I still hoped that I would connect with this baby I'd been carrying. I still don't feel like that baby I carried is the baby I have now, it doesn't feel like I have a link between the two.

I know the health visitor was worried about postnatal depression. I would say I'm not that bad now, I'm functioning, but I'm not happy. I had expectations of moments of joy, but they're not really there. I have had periods of depression in my life, darker times, but I feel like I'm more on a flat line now, more stable, secure. I know I wouldn't want to change anything, so I guess that's the best for me. I

feel like I'm watching my up and downs, but not getting pulled into them. I've been reading a lot, I look for the books that allow the range of what you might be feeling.
Interview with C, son 4 months

My life changed forever the instant my first baby was born. In one day, I went from defining myself as a 'career woman' to a 'full-time mum' – with no warning, training, understanding, insight, or support from family or friends. I now realise what I experienced was a shattering identity crisis, and a total lack of preparation, relevant skills and strategy for dealing with it.

I was completely cut off from my existing friendship group of work colleagues the moment I left my office environment the week before the birth. Although it was a busy office, I don't remember any female colleagues with children. They were all young, childless, or men with kids who were cared for in a way that didn't impact on their working hours, and we all worked full time, 9.00am to 6.00pm. As I'd moved to London for work, I had no other friends who lived close by and I didn't know my neighbours. I wasn't close with my mum or sisters; and even though both my siblings had children, we had never talked about anything personal, and our career and life choices, and responses to motherhood, were very different. I felt alone, friendless, isolated and bereaved of my previous life.

My partner and I muddled along over the first year. I was extremely sleep-deprived, and neurotic, demanding, moody and aggressive. He is amazing and stuck by me through this onslaught; but he carried on working and had his normal routine outside of our home life, and I'm guessing this is how he kept his sanity.

After a full year of feeling deeply sad, choked and wanting to cry a lot of the time – and not understanding why because I had everything I could possibly wish for: a healthy family, supportive partner and a comfortable home – I eventually plucked up the courage, and the organisation, to go to my GP and ask for counselling.

The biggest problem this presented was how to get an hour (plus travel time) per week with my daughter in childcare, where I felt confident she would be happy and safe, so I could attend the meetings. I had never had a break from full-time childcare as I felt I had no one to turn to. My partner worked full time with no chance of asking for leave, and I couldn't bring myself to impose my needs on anyone I'd met locally, as they all had small children, too. There was no question of my child going into a nursery, as the imagery of abandoning my child to experience any of the feelings of isolation that I had myself was too painful.

In the end, I asked my sister who lived locally to take my baby so I could 'have a break' – but reaching out and asking for this help from the family I felt emotionally cut off from was a huge deal for me, and actually making it happen was a massive step towards coming out of depression.

The NHS provided six sessions with a counsellor, who was basically competent and helped me get back on track; but following a further year of counselling when the depression returned after my second child, I now understand the issues upsetting me went much deeper, further back, and needed a lot more unravelling than I realised at that time.

I still feel very sad and choked with emotion when I see a vulnerable woman's friends give her small acts of kindness. It's such a powerful thing to do for someone. I so badly wanted to be cared for and nurtured at that time, and I felt so alone and friendless. I now realise I had fallen into a child-like state, and it had tapped into an old childhood feeling of abandonment and wanting my emotions to be cared for that I had experienced when I was growing up and had never acknowledged, understood or healed.

It has taken me seven years of hard work, both physically caring for my children and mentally caring for myself, to get through the huge change that I faced from the day of my first child's birth. I recently completed a course to learn to be a doula to help support other women in having a loving, instinctive

Photo: Kerry Ghais

birth experience, and feel cared for throughout their pregnancy and postnatal time; but it also offered me a therapy and re-birth for myself. I reflected on my whole journey into motherhood, and everything I have learned about my life history and personal psychology on the way, and how this will influence my family's future.
Anonymous

Primip

Who speaks of the fear and rage that burn
in a new mother's mind's eye,
behind bashful smiles, weary groans and coy pride?
Who sees her sleep-eluded;
high on adrenalin, duty and grief
attending her precious little thief;
an intruder perverting all her known beliefs?
Who sees the white-hot rage writhing and wailing,
wanting to shake, squeeze and smother?

Who speaks of how much they understood
the poor lass that flew from a bridge
with her precious mewling child held close,
her love impassioned and devout?
No pretty crinoline to billow and slow;
to parachute their pace towards the bank
as Sarah Henley gratefully there once had.

Nearly two weeks in
the health visitor breezed by
for a second and final visit.
'So how are you doing?'
Apropos of complete dishonesty
she contrived jocular disbelief; 'Well, she's still alive'
and concocted a confident smile to good effect,
before offering a cup of tea;
presenting as worthy, capable and kind; just SO tired.

She knew it best to keep very schtum
over the prevailing hum that rattled
in her head as they were nattering
and guessed it wise not to mention
so many things that were really mattering.
She proved capable of ticking the boxes
to secure an acceptable Edinburgh score.

Her blood lumpy and insufficient
from the inertia of anaemia, and feeding
she would trace the transit of clots upwards,
awaiting their arrival in her chest,
growing confused at each continuing breath
as days made weeks then milestones.
She would continue in this vein of belief;
musing over getting her limited affairs in order
and taking selfies for posterity
while outlining the origin of some cancer;
envisaging its edges expanding inside her,
rapidly retiring her from her grief
and orphaning the beast.

She festered on her end of the sofa,
loose of skirt, in lanolin-smeared feeding top,
cold coffee beside herself,
breast pump groaning on loop; taunting –
inciting her to throw it to the wall –
as lumps of lochia loosened
and seemed to laugh
with the lingering scent of labour
as they left her.
A dirty patio pane divided her
from other people's summer;
a smeared constant confirming
how useless she could be.

The noise of the fans fatigued her as she
fought oxytocin fugues to rise
and honour the infant's various cries.
She marvelled at how she continually knew how to do
but could never countenance what or who to be,
as so many things remained the same
but everything was irrevocably changed.
Claire Robinson

You can still feel quite down

All those comments people make to pregnant women really drive me crazy, like, 'Oh, get your sleep now.' You can't conceive what it's going to be like when you're pregnant. It's so overwhelming. I said to a friend of mine that I would never regret it, but I now understand why people may not want to have a baby, which I didn't before, because it is so consuming.

And yet you love your child so much, but you can still feel really quite down at the same time. And you can't cheer yourself up by taking yourself off to the cinema or something – you've still got someone who's reliant on you.

I remember going to see a friend of mine years ago who had two gorgeous children, lovely husband, lovely house and she was depressed, and I remember thinking, 'Why are you depressed? You've got everything,' but now I understand.

Interview with G, daughter 14 months

This has a happy ending. I promise
Suddenly finding myself at my graduation ceremony, pregnant.

Sitting opposite a counsellor listening to her say, 'Spend some time thinking about keeping it' whilst I instinctively laid my hands on my tummy communicating with what lay inside already.

I'd always been maternal, the one at parties as a child wanting to play with the baby.

Standing in the dark, alone on a cliff by Brighton Marina in the middle of the night, contemplating jumping off.

Lying on the cold hard pavement in Kemptown being kicked in the side of the ribs repeatedly.

My front door being smashed in and being accused of flirting at a party when some guy was just being nice, and then being interrogated all night.

A friend coming back to my flat to survey the damage when he smashed up my flat as he had become suspicious I had kept a 'secret' from him, and he flew into a jealous red-eyed rage (before finding out that I had just made him a lovely birthday cake).

Feeling ashamed and guilty every time I went back to him after attempting to break free, when my patient and loyal friends found out.

One of the hardest decisions I've ever had to make is to have an abortion whilst being in a domestic violent relationship with a man who was about to have a baby with his ex-partner (or not so 'ex' as it turned out).

The anguish and sense of loss of saying goodbye to a potential life, whilst my partner was busy preparing for a new arrival and then welcoming her into the world.

Now I look back and think of myself as a survivor.

I did have that abortion, I eventually left that man, although it took me three years; and now, over 20 years on, I have a loving, caring partner and three beautiful children, and I live a creative and mostly happy life.

Thanks to some very old friends, my mum, going to therapy and some (thankfully) inner resilience, I managed to scrape up some self-esteem and save myself from a relationship that could have possible ended my life, or at least severely damaged my mental health and brought a child into the world with a legacy of abuse, conflict and misery.

My children are not let down by their dad, they don't feel scared and they love him, and we all feel loved. So, although having an abortion was such an awful thing to go through, and she/he would have been over 20 now, I don't regret that decision. I look at my children now and feel grateful that I waited and gave them a lovely daddy, and a good start in life… and I feel safe.

Anonymous. Dedicated to K.L, H.S & M.A

Pushing myself
I've always been quite hard on myself. Like, 'Come on, you gave birth a whole week ago now – go to Asda!' Why? Going to Asda at any time is horrible; with a newborn baby, when you're feeling vulnerable, like you've been in a six car pile-up, why would you do that to yourself? There's part of me that's really horrible to myself.

Interview with A, daughter 6 months

At the beginning, I couldn't cope. My partner would come in; I'd hand her to him, rush off to the bathroom, sit there on the floor bawling my eyes out. They say play with your child, but she'd be just lying there not doing anything because she's a baby. I'd got a teddy on the back of the chair and I'd be trying to make up this story for her: there's this lion on the

mountain (which is the chair) and an elephant sucking water up from a lake. And I said, 'She's not doing anything.' He's like, 'She's a week old, what do you expect?'
Interview with B, daughter 15 months

A difficult year

LittleOne is one year old now. This year has been tough. Although LittleOne was an easy baby, much easier than his brother at the same age, juggling two children, while recovering after giving birth, being sleep-deprived, and – in my case – in a new town where I did not have a support network, was extremely challenging.

Many days, I felt trapped, bored of the endless routine of the newborn but not strong enough to do anything else. I almost never saw my husband – most days I was in bed when he came home from work. When my energy level went up a bit, I wanted to do more; but I was still constrained by the children, their timetable, their bedtime, and I still needed to go to bed early anyway, and got frustrated. I tidied up the house, I read books, I tried to meet the mums from the NCT class, but they seemed to be always busy when I wasn't.

The truth is that I craved real human interactions, with someone who would actually listen to me, at a deep level. I'm not one for small talk, and I was suffering. Children are amazing, but not enough. A couple of months before returning to work, I found out about Mothers Uncovered and I joined a writing course.

Those mornings were great: it was a group of women who were there to listen to each other, focusing on the mum, not the babies, and I loved every moment of it.

With my return to work, things changed: I now have more time on my own, and I love feeling like myself again. I'm older, more tired, my pelvic floor will never be the same again, and often I have breakfast with my sons at 6.00am, and when I get to work it's already been a long day; but, despite the contradictions and the constraints that make my life, I'm happy.
Chiara Corrao

A fear of taking it out on her

My life has changed completely; I think there's a lot expected of mothers to be this angelic-type person. When you do feel upset or emotional, you're not supposed to be feeling this way. It is known that mothers suffer from depression, that is publicised, but they talk about that straight after you've had a baby. A year later you're a bit out on your own. I spoke to a friend and said, 'I'm really not coping at the moment, but can't put my finger on it,' and she said, 'I'm feeling exactly the same.' I think there's not enough support around for when you go back to work and you have to juggle the stresses of work with looking after a baby. It's not like when you've just had the baby – your baby gets older but you still don't have the freedom. You can't run around and go out like you used to.

It's the mood stuff that's most difficult, and not wanting to take things out on her, being afraid of things like that happening. There was an incident in the middle of the night when I was upset – I thought I'd breastfeed her to sleep because she woke up. I think I created the situation because I was in a bad mood. She kept fidgeting, and I was yelling out, 'No!' and shaking my whole body; so of course she started crying, and I felt really bad because I'd got upset and that affected her, and I felt terrible that I'd made her cry when she hadn't done anything. It's the lack of sleep thing – you're so exhausted you could go to sleep standing up. Sleep deprivation is scary because it brings out sides of you you'd never seen. I would never ever harm my child, but I have more of an understanding as to why someone would. The thought that it goes through your head is horrifying.

Issues to do with my emotional rollercoaster have been quite pivotal to myself as a mother. I've found it really hard to look forward to things because you never know what the day's going to be like. But as she grows older, she does so much more, so much interaction. It's easy to whinge about the negative things, but sometimes the rewards are almost intangible – it's hard to put into words what it feels like when you baby smiles at you or gives you a kiss.

Photo: Kerry Ghais

She's the light of my life, the joy of watching her. Seeing her smiling face in the morning. When she started walking confidently – which is only in the last few weeks – seeing her little body walking through our kitchen. Patting her dolly and rocking it. I really feel we're a proper family unit now. Having that Sunday to go and do family things. As she gets older, to be able to experience your childhood again. All the fun things you used to do, to get to do them again. I don't know how you put into words what I've gained, but they all add up.

Interview with G, daughter 14 months

Screaming

She has colic, so a day where we don't have four hours of continuous crying is a good day. A

good day would be only two hours. Or no hours. Of colic crying, anyway, which is a very different sort of crying. It's not the 'I need changing or feeding' cry, it's a hysterical, 'There's nothing you can do to comfort me.' We have had a couple of days like that recently and I don't know why. I've read everything I can about it. I've changed my diet, given up dairy, caffeine, alcohol, breathing… it feels like sometimes I've given up so much, all I'm eating is dry toast.

The days when she hasn't been like that are heaven, she's a different child. And those days seem more manageable. The colic started at around three weeks and probably peaked at six weeks. The days she has it, it's hours of screaming, we spend a lot of time pacing the

Photo: Kerry Ghais

floor. The doctor and the health visitor said there's nothing we could do, it'll pass. In fact, the health visitor wasn't particularly helpful. She said, 'If that's all you have, it's not that bad.'

My husband bounced on the bed with her for about an hour, it was the only way he could get her to be quiet. It's heart-breaking. I had some very distressing conversations with him about it, he was seeing it as her being a naughty baby. It wasn't my idea of motherhood. It makes you feel inadequate, that she's so unhappy. I'd wanted to be a mother for so long, I had these images of staring down at her cot, putting a kiss on her forehead and everything would be lovely; but it's more walking round a darkened house with her yelling. My mum said, 'Any challenges you come up against in the future, just compare it to that – you can't scare me, I've had a child with colic.'

We have had some lovely days, though. It's appreciating the good things: she smiles, she gurgles, she talks and, this week, she's

shaking her head and sucking her thumb. It's balancing it. She can't help it. It's the colic, not her. And now her personality is developing, my husband can see it too now when she smiles at him.

I feel quite exposed because of the hormones. The tears come quicker than they've ever done before; I don't like people seeing it, but it's so hard to control. I feel a lot more vulnerable. I went to see my doctor, who suggested I might have postnatal depression. I think it was just I hadn't slept, we all had colds. It felt like that was a label that was being put on me. I don't think I have depression.

I feel very bonded with her. I can get up every day and do the things I need to do. It's just this is tough. You do have bad days and you do need to cry. You have to let it out.

There are good days. I've got a little clip on my phone of her cooing and gurgling at my husband – I play it all the time, it's the cutest thing. I'm so in love with her. She's perfect. We've got issues, but she's perfect. She's very serious and thoughtful when she meets new people, she takes her time doing things. She could never fail. Whatever she does, I'd be proud of her.

My mum is amazing, so supportive and protective. When I was little, I had a dairy intolerance. She's been so sympathetic about pacing the floor and stuff. She offers to hold her, too. It's nice we've had something new to talk about. She didn't have any support when she had me. They'd moved area; she didn't know anyone; my dad wasn't hands-on. She was on her own. It made me feel confident to go off and do things – I was the first one in my family to go off to university. I've got a challenging job, too. She made me feel I could

do anything. It's not about money or material things, it's just about being there.

Most of my friends don't have children yet, and I feel a distance from them. And with my baby having colic, it's to do with my image of myself holding everything together and being perfect. I don't like the idea of people coming round and her screaming, I find it very stressful. The ones that do have children have been less pushy.

My husband knows when I'm near breaking point and he takes her – it's amazing. One night he got her quiet in her cot – I don't know how he did it – and we were sitting on the floor in the room playing Snap. It's brought us closer together – there's more love, we're both fascinated by her.

Interview with O, daughter 2 months

12. Loss

What bereavement means to mothers

Motherhood is a time of heightened emotions, and loss can be hard to bear. D talks about going into labour thinking she was having twins, but being told that one of her babies had died; she deals with coming to terms with the loss, her joy in her son, and her discovery of her own strength. Having a baby can also be a powerful reminder of those you have lost: Q, V and A talk about the loss of their own mothers. N describes the internal conflict of losing her father at the same time as having a baby. And Q suffered several miscarriages, which coloured her feelings when her friends discussed their pregnancies.

She looked like she was asleep

I'd been expecting twins. We'd had our first round of IVF treatment, and it had been a success. We had to do it privately because my husband already had grown-up children from his first marriage. I had two embryos planted in me. They both took, but one looked slightly different from the start. But as the pregnancy progressed, it looked normal, so it all seemed fine.

I was quite ill after the IVF, so I needed nine weeks off work. I had ovarian hyper-stimulation, when the ovaries go into overdrive from the drugs and keep producing hormones. My body fluid leaked into my abdominal cavities. I looked like I was eight months pregnant from early on. In four days, I gained 8kg. I couldn't breathe properly and was in hospital for three weeks. Once I had recovered from the drugs, I really enjoyed being pregnant, and I missed that once I'd given birth.

We got to the 12-week and the 20-week scans, and they were both ok. I was being scanned more frequently because it was twins. At 28 weeks, they noticed one was growing less well. They were monitoring me weekly and

checking the blood flow. At 30 weeks, I had another scan. They said I needed to be delivered because the blood flow wasn't good. I was worried, but we had to go with it. I had great faith in my consultant. It was a balancing act because they were twins. If it had been a single baby, they would have delivered without question. They might even have delivered at 28 weeks.

We were excited, a bit panicked. We were totally disorganised at home because we had thought we had ten weeks to go. I was still at work. I had to email the office from the clinic on my Blackberry and say my maternity leave was starting now. I went into the hospital over the weekend to have steroid injections to mature their lungs. We were told they'd be in intensive care after the birth.

We had a 10.30am slot booked in the theatre on Monday morning. All the doctors and nurses were there because with twins you need two midwives, two paediatricians. Then the consultant did a scan and they couldn't find one heartbeat. I was in an admissions room, next to a woman in the early stages of labour, when they came out and said that one of my babies had died. I wasn't in a private room, because I thought I was just about to go into theatre. The caesarean was cancelled.

I had more scans to check the other one was ok. That was probably the most distressing part because I had to go down to the antenatal clinic – firstly into the parents' room, where I knew you went to be given bad news, then to be scanned. That sound of the Doppler machine still freaks me out because I associate it with losing one twin. Thankfully, they turned the sound off; I couldn't look at the screen. I didn't want to see the other baby. He seemed fine – there were two separate placentas.

It was decided we wouldn't deliver that day because he was all right. The aim was to get him another two weeks and get him bigger. So we went home and had to tell the family the news – it was a real mixed emotions day. Trying to be strong for each other and deal with our emotions of loss.

The next day, we went back to the hospital early. After the scan, they were very honest and frank. They said his blood flow was beginning to dip. We went into another room while the consultants had a discussion. Then they said they thought we should deliver him that day. I'd eaten breakfast so we had to wait six hours. I felt a bit detached. I was shaking with nerves and from the drugs.

We had a discussion about our daughter – did we want to see her, how did we want to see her? She was delivered at 3.10pm and he was at 3.11pm. He cried, which was good because we'd been told not to expect that. They whisked him off. They brought her round so we could hold her. We spent a lot of time with her. She was like a tiny dolly. She looked like she was asleep, she was perfect. We hadn't finally decided on their names because we didn't know what we were having; but we wanted to establish them as personalities, not just the live one and the dead one.

I was in a room that wasn't used very often for patients – people kept coming in looking for things. That was my birthday as well. Someone came in and said, 'Oh you've got a lot of stuff, what's all this?' It was the memory boxes they give you if a baby dies.

I burst into tears and said, 'All I want to do is have a bath, get this catheter out and get into the room.' My partner had gone home for a while so I was on my own. I wanted to be able to go upstairs and see my son without the catheter, actually walk up there. They sorted it out and I got into the private room. It was about 10.00pm that evening that I went up to see him in his incubator, lying stretched out with his breathing tubes, looking very relaxed, almost like he was lying on the beach.

We had a postmortem for our daughter and a funeral. Lots of ceremonies. The team were keen to have a postmortem because they wanted to learn. I wanted it, too, so that I could understand. It revealed that the placenta was full of clots and thickened walls, it wasn't functioning properly. The drugs I was on were anti-clotting, so it probably kept the pregnancy going on longer than nature would have.

Our son came home after a few weeks. Because he was in special care, we were able to go out and have a drink. I had the best babysitters in the world. And I was able to sleep and recover. I was able to express milk easily for him. I stayed in the flat at the hospital to feed him during the day. Although I was called 'mum', I didn't feel like it because I couldn't pick him up and care for him. I wanted to, but there was a fear there because he was so small. I had the first cuddle when he was still quite small – he had his tubes in still – but he was stable enough to come out of the incubator.

Bringing him home was quicker than we thought. They needed the bed. On the way down in the lift, I burst into tears because I didn't quite believe, I hadn't let myself believe that we would get to that point. The lift felt very significant because we had always been going up and down at significant points. It was the start of our family life.

We had a bit of a laugh trying to get the car seat in. It wasn't even our car seat because we thought we'd have another week. We'd placed an order of two of everything, which we'd had to cancel; then re-ordered, which we'd only just done, because it felt symbolic. We went to our neighbours, who'd been very supportive. They'd put balloons on the door, and we celebrated his homecoming with them. We had our daughter's funeral after he was home and celebrated her – it felt like closure.

I've learned that I'm very strong, that I can deal with the unexpected, a very emotional situation. I've been tested, and sometimes I'm amazed I've been able to deal with it. It wasn't motherhood as I'd expected it, but we feel it's ok. It was meant to be. You don't know how it will be with IVF – I had two embryos put back in me, but the outcome could be either two babies, or one, or none; so we had a positive result. All along our hope was to have one healthy baby, which we have. If our daughter had survived, she might not have been healthy; I'd rather she died in me and not in the incubator.

Interview with D, son 4 months

I drove straight from hospital to hospice

At 37 weeks pregnant, I found out my dad had only a short time to live. He was young, in his 50s. It felt like I was under unbelievable pressure to have the baby before he died. I had to go through extreme sadness and extreme happiness at the same time. And I couldn't postpone one – they had to both happen at the same time.

It had been quite a stressful pregnancy. Earlier on, I'd thought he would have the treatment and get well, then I'd be able to have the baby; but it didn't work out like that. Everything changed forever, within a few weeks. Tragedy does that to you and motherhood. Before, I felt I was very much in the daughter role; then suddenly I was a mother and had another person to look after – it felt like I was trying to combine both.

I took some decisions I would never have anticipated. I decided to be induced when I went slightly over my due date so that my daughter and dad could meet. It always felt like I was juggling two things. I just felt this extreme urgency and pressure to get back to my dad, because every day was precious. I put the pressure on myself, but I could feel it from everybody. He was so excited to meet his grandchild.

My birth wasn't too bad, considering what I've heard from other people. I should have stayed in longer, but I drove straight from the hospital to the hospice. We had a few weeks of this strange life – a new life and a life that was about to end. Every day I'd drive there, having had hardly any sleep. He had his own room, so we could be a family in there, but it felt like I was always trying to keep her quiet – it didn't feel right to have a screaming baby near all these people who were dying. He held her every day and we had these lovely family moments. We've got photos which are beautiful, but so sad because he's so ill in them. He doesn't look like my dad. He never got to see me as a mum. I like to think he's looking down on me and watching me, but it's hard to know what I believe. It feels hard to know he'll never see her grow up.

My partner is amazing. We've been together a long time and were quite young when we met. He saw my dad as more than a father-in-law because we grew up together. My mum also had cancer in her 40s, so it feels like I've parented them both at some point. Even though I'm a mum, I still want my parents. I do feel grateful for the time I had with my dad.

My relationship with my family has got stronger, but there's a massive void now. My brothers and I are creating babies, but it doesn't fill the void. It feels frightening to have just one parent, especially as she's been ill too; although she's healthy now, thankfully. I feel angry sometimes at other people, like my in-laws, who are still alive and are able to be part of her life. I don't tell them, obviously – it's internalised.

I feel like I entered my pregnancy with a lot of issues, and just had others added to the list. I can talk to other people about their first weeks of motherhood, but I don't have the same story. I gave up breastfeeding, and I haven't come to terms with it. I still feel very embarrassed when I take out a bottle. I was very passionate about wanting to breastfeed, but I wasn't in a relaxed, calm environment to establish it. I had to make my dad the priority because each day might have been the last. I still feel a failure, though, and I feel incredibly

Photo: Kerry Ghais

jealous of the other women in the group who are able to breastfeed. I never live up to the expectations I set myself. I think what's happened will shape me for the rest of my life.

My daughter is a huge comforter and motivator. The first time I was alone with her at home was when she was eight weeks old. My fear was that I'd go into a spiral of grief and I wouldn't bond with her because of it, but I think I have. I don't want to transfer those feelings to her because I know she's receptive to my emotions and state of mind. I want her to know it's ok to feel, though.

I have such a strong, all-encompassing bond with her. I feel like I've always wanted to be a mum, it's at the core of me. I'm not as anxious as I anticipated about doing everything right. We're just muddling through and that seems to be ok. I feel we're a little team.

I do feel I really understand how precious life is and how everything can change in a second. It gives me an urgency to do everything quickly because my dad's life was shortened and other things happened to my family. I'm almost desperate to have another child so I can do it differently the next time, but I feel like I'm waiting for the next thing to happen. I feel the need to control what's uncontrollable sometimes, but I'm really learning to be in the present with her and not be thinking forwards or backwards all the time. A baby's life is simplicity, and my life feels complicated.

Interview with N, daughter 3 months

It's hard if people tell you they're pregnant

Most of my friends have children; I was one of the last in the group to have kids, and I was aware of that. A few don't want them, and a few others are having difficulty. I miscarried, and it's really hard every time someone tells you they're pregnant. My miscarriages were over a couple of years, and the last one I had was two years before I had him. I never begrudged anyone their children, but it's still a sad experience.

I always hoped there would be a baby but I couldn't say for sure. There was no confidence for me and I didn't ever want to take anything

for granted, that's the key thing, but I allowed myself to keep on hoping.

Interview with Q, son 4 months

Losing my mother

It's made me think about my mum a lot, as she died three years ago from breast cancer; so it's obviously made me reflect a lot on her not being around. I was really worried that I'd get postnatally depressed because I thought it might hit me all over again, but it hasn't done that. It has made me feel sad thinking about how things might have been. I see my dad quite a lot, but I know my mum would be really hands on. Just things like I'd have gone round, and she'd have grabbed him and made me a cup of tea, or got me some lunch or something. When I was listening to music when I was pregnant, like if I was driving to work, I'd get very tearful. That's partly the pregnancy hormones, and obviously music can be quite emotive, but I feel I've got more of an understanding of how she would have felt being a mum to me; so I feel a closeness, even though she's not here. She would have just adored him.

I'm doing my best, and I'm quite often thinking of ways she brought me up and I'm trying to do the same, not to the letter, but certain things I'm doing. People can be really judgmental about mums so I'm not being judgmental of other people. But, for instance, my mum didn't really like dummies, and lots of friends have got their babies to sleep with a dummy but I never use one for that reason…

Although me and my mum didn't have loads of conversations about babies, as I wasn't in that stage at the time, she said she really enjoyed breastfeeding me and my brother, so I wanted to do that. I see how my brother brings up his children and I think he really bears some of that in mind, too, and I respect how they're turning out.

My brother's children are young; he lives in Brighton. I'm close to my brother, but we're completely polar opposites and I think we've got closer since having children. He's a few years older, so that gap was quite big at one point but not so big now. We don't really talk about our mother together – I'm someone that likes to talk about things, whereas he's someone who really doesn't. He wasn't as close to her – they got on really well but I think it's just like a mother-daughter thing. I spent a lot of time with her and he used to live in London, so I was closer to her.

Interview with V, son 8 months

My mum died 12 years ago. The worst of the grief is over. When you lose a parent, it's incredibly shocking, no matter what your relationship with them was. My relationship with her was quite difficult, we were quite enmeshed. She had a lot of issues. She died when I was 29 so we didn't get a chance to sort it all out. We had a nice patch when she was ill and I was looking after her, but we never got to be mates or to have a relationship where I trusted her.

Sometimes, I have this vision of her coming into my life and taking the baby, and telling me I'm doing it all wrong. I have very visual daydreams, so I can see the whole thing happening, even though I'm awake. I told a friend about it the other day and she looked really shocked. She said she thought I was really close to my mother. And I kind of was, but I can't imagine it as good. I wonder if it's a way of coping – to make it seem bad so you don't miss it.

I've thought about her every day at some point since I became a mother, and it's always bad things. I see her thinking, 'She's your nemesis, she's exactly what you deserve. She's a real handful – well, you know, that's what I had to go through.'

There's always a real kickback – I'm never going to do what my mum did to me, but already I can feel myself doing those things. I can actually appreciate her anxiety, she was a very nervous person. It's interesting to start to dare to look at what I could have had with her around, me being older and more mature and her being a lovely grandmother. Every night we say, 'God bless Granddad and Nonna in heaven.'

Mum would have loved that. She was so full of life and creativity. I can feel the things she would have liked and I kind of do them inadvertently as well. If I think about it too much, I get worried and think, 'Are all mother/daughter relationships doomed...?' I try and think about her separately as a woman, not just my mum. I try to call her by her name.

Interview with A, daughter 6 months

My mum died ten years ago. It seems such a long time, but it doesn't, as the actual time of her death is still so vivid in my mind. The overwhelming thing is the fact that she was desperate to have grandchildren. So she's missed out, and so will he. I suppose I have a slight sense of her, but not as much as I thought I would. It's just quite a difficult one because she'd have been such a good granny. There's no grandparents on my partner's side who live locally. My dad's seen us a few times and he phones to see how we are. But he doesn't say a lot, like a lot of dads. I'm close to my sister, so we can support each other over that.

Interview with Q, son 4 months

13. Hopes and fears

... and anxiety and vivid dreams

Hopes and fears for the future can be intense for parents, and, for some, are overwhelming. Many report anxiety and intense dreams, and the burden of responsibility can weigh heavily. 'I tried going to bed once without checking on her and I was up about ten minutes later, panicking even more than I was before,' says B.

My dreams are wild, vivid and full of my fears, which have increased since becoming a mother.
From 'Your Stories'

Hopes

I honestly, since having her, can't understand anyone who is pushy with their children or want them to 'be' something. I just couldn't care less; as long as she's happy, whatever kind of life she chooses. It makes me not understand more when parents ostracise their children for things like whether they're gay, or whether they choose a partner from a different religion. What does it matter? Just happiness and health are what matter. I'd like her to have a happy and easy life, and I don't care how that happens – whether she's interested in academic stuff, or jobs and careers; or if she's not and wants to have a family, and that makes her happy. It doesn't even cross my mind to worry about it. I don't want to be pushy, that's what I want to avoid. I know it's tempting to want your children to be in the best schools, and the best this and that, but I want her to find her own way, really, and not feel that pressure to do well. At the end of the day, it makes no difference.

I wasn't put under particular pressure growing up. My husband was, and that didn't do him any favours at all. My parents wanted me to do well, but they were like, 'Try your best and that will be fine.' I don't know if that's what makes me be

like that for the same reason. It's not something that really occurs to me. I just wouldn't want her to be in a situation where she feels unhappy or sad, as people do find their way in life. Things like that don't really matter as much as you think they do at the time.
Interview with R, daughter 6 months

I know she would benefit from a brother or sister, but I know that's not a given. I hope I'm giving her enough to grow up and make the most of her life, and be a decent person. And also to understand what we've achieved for her. It would be nice if she liked me and we had a good relationship.
Interview with I, daughter 4 months

I don't care what she wants to do. I want her to succeed, have a career mind, because it wasn't a major thing in my life. I want her to make a lot of friends, coming round any day of the week; I want her to have people around her, lots of support. And lots of friends.
Interview with J, daughter 7 months

Fears

I have lots of fears: that I won't be any good, that she won't be happy or healthy. That she won't love me, that she'll be bullied at school. The thoughts don't stay there, though – I'm too tired.
Interview with O, daughter 2 months

Photo: Cécile Chevalier

I worry about something happening to him at school, even though that's years away. Everything I think of in the future now involves him. What will HE be doing, when I'm doing that?
Interview with L, son 7 months

I wonder what sort of person she will become. I had a dream recently that she was a nightmare teenager. It might be because I'm a secondary school teacher. I know how great teenagers can be, but how difficult as well. I dreamt of doors smashing and, 'Oh I hate you, you don't understand me.'
Interview with M, daughter 9 weeks

When she was little, the older lot would say when she was crying, 'Oh does mummy hit you, does she smack you?' And it's, 'No,

mummy bloody well doesn't smack you.' But if you were out in town and someone said that, then social services might get involved. They think it's all right for them to say that.
Interview with B, daughter 15 months

I've definitely changed since she's come along. It's just the realisation of such a huge responsibility and this person who you love so much, and the thought of anything bad happening to them. It's the worry and the guilt you have, which is obviously normal and understandable – you can't be as worry-free as you were, or as chilled out.

Even stupid things, like going in the car; or like when I went to a theme park with my brother and sister recently. So it's not really about the baby, but general worries about life, and I find that's the biggest thing. It's hard to let go of that. You suddenly realise all the things that could go wrong in life; it sounds quite morbid, really. Before, I thought all that stuff was really far in the future, but when you have a baby, suddenly you've got this responsibility; it's terrifying and amazing at the same time, it's just sort of an awareness that wasn't really there before.

Actually, she is such a chilled-out baby and she sleeps so well, so it hasn't affected my day-to-day life as much as I had expected it to. She's been very easy as babies go, so that's been quite a surprise. So she fitted in around my general life quite well – it's more a mental thing, really.

Interview with R, daughter 6 months

On health

I have more nightmares than dreams now, there's bloody loads of them. It's like panic, something's going wrong. I go out and think she's in the car, and I turn around and she's not there – I've left her; I don't know where, she's just not in the car. I look in the boot, as well. It's quite strange. I'm overtired. It's like that list you get. It's the baby; then the partner; then the housework, the garden, the dog; everything, and you're about 20th on the list; you think, 'Ooh, can I just sit down and have a cup of tea…?'

I was sitting downstairs one day and I was like, something's wrong, something's wrong. Before that I'd never… I know I'm her mum, but I still can't believe I'm her mum. It's still quite, 'Shit, I'm a mum.' I was watching TV. It was 10.00pm and I was about to go to bed, anyway. I went up and she was like, 'Erp, erp' with her breathing. I picked her up and she wasn't herself. She was crying. She couldn't breathe and her throat had swollen up. I tried calming her down. I phoned the NHS number and they said take her up to the hospital. She ended up with steroids and nebulisers and asthma pumps. We were up there quite a long time. She'd had a reaction to something and her throat had swollen, all her larynx had swollen, she had a chest infection. She just couldn't breathe. She was crawling up me because she didn't like the doctor, she was

screaming. Oh, it was horrible. And we got back and she was alright, thank God.

Something I wouldn't say to my partner – I think it's just you don't want to admit it yourself – is I hate checking on her when she's asleep because I think she's dead. That whole cot death thing is drummed into you at the hospital. I'll go in, and I'll watch to see if her chest is going up and down – can I hear her breathing? It petrifies me. I'll wake up and I'll have to prod her just to see if she's still alive. He'd probably think it was daft.

Because she's the most precious thing and I really can't lose her, that's why I haven't been able to let anyone look after her for more than an hour. I can't cope because I might be losing her. I spoke to some other mums, and apparently it's quite normal to rush up and check on them. I tried going to bed once without checking on her and I was up about ten minutes later, panicking even more than I was before. It's one of the things that's normal that the women don't tell the blokes about. They don't say why particularly, but they just don't want to upset them, put that thought into their mind.

Interview with B, daughter 15 months

He had really bad wind, but I hadn't realised because it gradually built up. I thought he was hungry because he was really unsettled. I got myself in a right tizzy. For two or three nights, I don't think we had a wink of sleep. I'd had an argument with my now ex-partner, his dad, and I'd kicked him out. That was my worst moment – I'd got a bottle for him – it was the middle of the night. I was so frustrated not knowing what the problem was. I'd gone out and bought that heavy duty milk to try to make him sleep. He wasn't interested, I didn't know what to do with him.

I had all the emotional stuff going on, feeling on my own. I was doing one formula feed because my nipples were so sore, and that was my emotional crutch. I'm still feeling bad about it now, trying to justify why I gave him one lot of formula. I've not told anyone this, but I launched the bottle across the room because I was so fed up. I was a bit ashamed, you don't want to feel like you're losing it. Then I used some Infacol and it settled down within a day or so. I had to go round to my neighbour's and sleep during the day because I needed some emotional support.

I think the knowledge of dangers happening to your child comes with experience. I don't think instinct is the same as that experience. Accidents happen, though. On one occasion, he went tumbling down the stairs. I'd put him on the floor and gone to wash my hands, and I hadn't put the stair gate across. It was only a moment. I felt, 'I've not been on the ball for 30 seconds and this has happened.' I phoned the doctor and they told me to take him to A&E. So I did, and I had four doctors check him over. He was fine.

Interview with F, son 17 months

Anxiety daydream

Travelling downhill in a rush. It's not walking, but it's not running either. It's this particular way of staying vertical while falling forwards. The things I remember: the thud of the soles of my feet reverberating in my chest, the ridges of the rubber bar gripped in my hands, the sweat under the wool of my too warm coat, the running of my nose I didn't have time to stop and wipe.

My beautiful girl asleep in her pram. Her big, round, red cheeks, the left one tilted up at me. Her dark lashes resting on the tops of them. Her little nose.

There snuggled in her sheepskin. Green woollen blanket. Yellow babygro. Lilac flower motif. Amber necklace. Toe nails need cutting. Hands done, little finger on right hand a bit jagged. Dry patch of skin above left eyebrow. Beautiful hair. My girl.

I don't know how fast you can go rushing downhill pushing a buggy. I guess that's the problem, you're not really pushing it. You're holding on.

It's this strange feeling of falling forwards and pulling backwards at the same time. Very confusing.

I became hyper-aware of my movements, my coordination. I became aware of how easy it would be for me to make a mistake right now. My clammy hands gripped the handle bar even harder. It's a white knuckle ride, I thought, telling the joke to my girl in my head.

I talk to her all the time, whether she can hear or not.

I started to panic about the buggy slipping out of my hands, I checked the road for traffic, evaluated the likelihood of the pram being hit by a car should it slip away.

I saw it go in my mind, zooming away from me. I gripped harder.

I didn't see it go. I think I did, but I can't have. It must be what I thought I'd see. Though I can hear the turn of the wheels, the whip of the wind, see the shaking of her cheeks as it went over bumps. But I can't have. I can't have seen any of it.

I felt my cheek on the ground, the emptiness in my hands. Then my eyes pulled my head forward. I could see her. I could see her pram. It was on its side.

I do not know how long I did not see her for. How long I was not there. I hit my head.

The ground. Hit my head, tripped my foot. My hands. My hands let her go. I don't know.

I know that I had to be where I was going at 10.45am, I was running five minutes late.

I don't know how long it was until I knew the time again, every second has been a hundred years.

I crouched down to the pram. I looked under her blanket, under the sheepskin. A few seconds, hundreds of years. I moved very fast and I stood very still.

Listen. Listen for her. Nothing.

She was not there. Here. She is not here.

She is somewhere. She is. She is my little girl and she is somewhere.

I search. I search, I search. Everything. Everywhere. I see her.

Long hair. Dark lashes. Little nose. My little girl.

I look down. I see her, asleep in her pram.

Little nose, lashes resting on big red cheeks.

I keep going. I hold on. I don't let her go.

Rebecca Santos

14. Work-life balance

What happens when you have to go back?

Many women feel a conflict when it comes to time to go back to work, whether they are keen or not. There are some quite varied perspectives in this chapter – from Q, a silversmith who takes her child to work, 'The sound of me hammering comforts him,' to F, who is annoyed at media assumptions: 'I didn't necessarily want to have it all.'

Ambitions
I didn't want it to end like this
Ambiguous and clouded
Ambition with no home

I didn't want it to end like this
Tested and wrung out
Taking aim toward obscurity

I wanted more for you
Little one
Than borrowed arms and smiles
Whilst I fumble for definition in the grind

I didn't want it to end like this
A bundle cast asunder
For no good reason whatsoever

I didn't want it to end like this
I wanted to be sure of myself

So you could be sure of yourself

I wanted more for you
Little one
Than borrowed arms and smiles
While I fumble for definition in the grind
Gemma Painter

I don't want to go back
We'll have to move back to London next year with my husband's work. And then I'll have to go back to work. I'm enjoying being away from that, and don't like the thought of having to juggle work and daycare, with all my income going on that care. Part of work for me was going out after work, which I won't be able to do. I will feel like a grown-up. Like when you look at your parents when you're younger and can't imagine them ever having gone out.

My husband has said he'd like to be at home with her. We wouldn't want us both to be at work and not to see her, but we both have careers. It takes managing, but she comes first. I want her to grow up and see that's there's more to me than being a mother, so that she can see the choices for her. I was fairly successful at school and in my career, so it feels like people are looking at me thinking that I should know what to do, but I often don't have a clue.
Interview with I, daughter 4 months

Before she was born, I thought I'd definitely go back to work, but now I'm not sure. I didn't think I'd take to motherhood the way I have. I took her to work yesterday to show her off to the staff. It was nice visiting, but I didn't miss it.
Interview with M, daughter 9 weeks

He comes with me
My son comes to work with me and sleeps for some of it, other times he's there watching me in my workshop. I'm a silversmith and I have a

Photo: Kerry Ghais

studio. I know quite a lot of people who have brought their babies to work, and once it gets to a point when they're moving around, they use big playpens and stuff. The strange thing is, the sound of me hammering comforts him and sends him to sleep sometimes because he's used to hearing it, even from before he was born. He's talking to me quite a lot as well now, and he has been for quite some time. He's been making shapes with his mouth since he was about four weeks.

I would like to have more than one child, but I don't know whether, feasibly, I'll able to. It just changes everything, doesn't it? In terms of me carrying on working, it would make things more difficult. I'd like to have more for his sake, but I don't know.

It hasn't affected my work yet, but it's probably a bit too early to tell, as I've been working on commissions that have already been planned; but I haven't started any new work, so it will be interesting to see what comes out.

Interview with Q, son 4 months

You're never ready

I'm in my late 20s – my partner was thinking I'd want babies when I was older, but I met some career women in my job, who were late 40s, early 50s. One of them was saying how tired she was with a toddler, I genuinely thought she meant her grandchild, but it was her own child. She was saying how irritating it would be when the toddler was a teenager. I thought I couldn't be in my mid-60s with a teenager.

You don't realise your life is going past you. It would have been quite easy for me to have worked until I was 45 and then decided I wanted a child. I wouldn't have the energy. I don't have the energy now that I had ten years ago. At what point is it right to become a parent? You can never really feel ready for it, it just somehow comes into your line of vision at some point, and then it's pretty much all you can think about.

Interview with E, daughter 9 months

Got to keep up

You just want to achieve so much more. With my job, even though it's hard because I have to take time off at short notice if he's poorly or something – which is embarrassing and annoying for work – all that aside, I feel more focused. It's not just all about me. I've got to keep up with him. I need to get myself up-to-date, get a computer, get with technology for his sake. I'm still stuck in the last millennium. I keep up with my filing at home, and I'm doing a study skills course. Because I'm a single parent, I'm so responsible.

Interview with F, son 17 months

What am I to become?

One of my fears is, 'Who am I? As a mum. What am I to become?' I had grand plans of becoming a writer. Or a comedian. It could still happen, but I need the confidence to carry on with that, and the space to allow myself to do it. I feel far away from performing. I was supposed to do a gig last night, but I couldn't because my parter broke his arm. Part of me felt quite relieved I couldn't do it because I'd got scared again. We've postponed the gig. I want to be able to say to my daughter, 'You can do whatever you want to. It doesn't have to be a big thing – if you want to sing, or do politics or something.' I don't want her to say, 'Well what did you do?'

Interview with A, daughter 6 months

Tentatively dip my toe back

It took me a lifetime of education, studying, apprenticeships and work to fulfil my career ambitions; I feel there was very little in that trajectory that prepared me for the primal love I feel for my children, and these overwhelming urges to understand myself,

live a balanced lifestyle, and be the parent I want to be in the biggest job of all: bringing up the next generation in this world. I believe I have just lived through a crash-course in life skills for motherhood; the lessons I have learned are to remember I am evolved from many hard-working mothers, that I live in a natural world finely balanced to meet our needs, and to trust my instincts.

These are not skills I trained for or valued in my previous career, which was all about management, technology and storytelling; but now I have them, I can see how both attitudes and skill-sets complement each other, and I feel much better equipped for my future.

Now my children are old enough to go to school, I have built a network. I am ready to tentatively dip my toe back into my previous life and enter the career world again. I hope it will meet me halfway and allow me to be there for my family, as well as fulfil my work ambitions; but I will have to wait and see if society has caught up with my understanding of this now.

In an age of celebration of suffrage and feminism, will I be able to find the balance of work and home life that I crave, and bring up my daughters in a world which understands and values this necessity? I hope my children will embrace both the natural and the technological strengths our world has today, and find a path which celebrates and balances the two.

Anonymous

I didn't want to have it all

I get annoyed with the media that say it's so easy to become a mother and go back to work. It's not just the work – you've got a baby at home who's teething and waking you up at all hours. How can you be firing on all cylinders at work? I know we've realised we can't 'have it all'. I didn't necessarily want to have it all; I'd prefer not to have to work at the moment, but I don't have a choice. I'd love a happy family scenario, but maybe not that many women have that.

Interview with F, son 17 months

15. What's next?

Teenagers and more babies...

Mothers often find themselves panicking about the next stage in their child's life. Perhaps it is a way to manage the responsibility they feel. At Mothers Uncovered, we invite women to write a letter to themselves which is posted to them six months later, in which they can project a little in advance. In this chapter, Lesley Hughes and Maggie Gordon-Walker offer a glimpse into the next stages of motherhood – when your tiny baby turns into a tall teenager, and what happens when another one comes along.

Thirteen

When the baby arrives – immediately thrusting us into in a new paradigm, shattering all imaginings of how it may be, suddenly, finally, facing the actuality of the physical being that's been forming itself inside – all the guts and the glory of the valiant, intense labour melts away. There they are, right in front of us, innocence and purity personified, there to be utterly cared for, dependent upon us for survival.

I knew then, looking down at him, holding him, joyously, feeling the light weight of his little warm bundle, noticing my whole being flooding with love, that here was the greatest gift; and I instantly felt the confident uprising of the mama in me. Life was not going to be the same again.

And true to the nature of impermanence, where no state says the same, our little one, that we get into a rhythm with and way of being, changes! And changes. And keeps on changing and needing something different from us; and we must continuously adapt to their development – their emotional, physical, mental, soulful needs – to meet them, support them, attempt to understand them; and constantly train them to be in the world, in some kind of grounded and confident way, so

that eventually they won't need us to survive. And, if we have done a reasonable job, they may wish to spend some time with us, confide in and share with us, and be in our lives out of choice, and not obligation.

Thirteen years into this unimaginable, consuming parenting experience, I find myself living with a whole new incarnation of the little boy that I knew. There seemed to be a link between the baby, toddler, pre-schooler, infant, junior phases – a transition that was seemingly gradual. The skins kept shedding to reveal the next version of the one before, but this most recent phase is a shock to the system.

I suddenly realised one day when Louie was 12 that we were at eye-level – I was no longer looking down towards him, or had to bend to hug him. And then one day, very soon after, I was looking up to him. And I cried. It dramatically changed the dynamics between us. It's been just Louie and me since he was four, and, despite the changes, I knew my place with him; and he, I felt, knew his with me; and this physical change momentarily shook the confidence that I have always felt in my general ability to effectively parent him. Would he suddenly realise that, being bigger than me, he could use his stature to take

Lesley Hughes and .Maggie Gordon-Walker in a production of *Your Stories.*
Photo: Gideon Fisher

advantage of me, defy me, challenge me more than he would if he was still smaller than me? Would this alter how he saw me and how he saw himself with me? I suppose I was questioning how deep his respect for me went. There was some fear about what I may discover, and I was certainly shaken by the gatecrashing entrance of this potential game-changer. It felt like something settled and familiar had been abruptly snatched away.

I'm getting used to the physicality now, now that he's towering over me and can easily lift me; and, despite the fact that there is sometimes something of a battle of wills present between us that may erupt in a heated exchange with his deep voice, I do feel that he ultimately has true respect for me. Phew!

It's as if the little chap I knew so well has dissolved, and there is this startlingly different version in his place. I must admit, there is an element of the confused mind that so loves things to stay the same, wondering where that

little one went to. It's a kind of death. I will never see him again, never hold him again; and as with death, there is grief. I suppose it's a compounded grief for all those phases that passed before; and this stark difference is a wake-up call to the final departure of the infant and junior, and the simultaneous celebratory arrival and emergence of the teenager.

That dreamy notion to have a baby bears no resemblance to this. This is something else entirely.

I'm aware that those with older teens will say, 'Just you wait, you have no idea.' And it's true, we do have no idea about the challenges of any phase until it's actually happening; and all we can do is continue to commit to the role that we agreed to take on, digging ever deeper into our unknown repertoire of parenting skills and talents that seemingly can't be fully discovered until we fail, make so-called mistakes and behave badly. Hopefully, not just me?

This, right now, for me, is the most challenging to date, as I'm constantly shifting the balance of being there for him, with him, and backing off, depending on what is happening and how much I feel he silently needs me, and how much he wants space just to be who he is becoming without me.

I've always known that Louie was quite eccentric. A humorous chatterbox that pushes boundaries; a bright and entertaining communicator, able to confidently talk to anyone from such a young age, with curiosity way beyond his years, and who used to love to dress up flamboyantly at any opportunity. I have always delighted in this, and enjoyed all the fruits of parenting such an energetic and expressive character; and I often wondered how this would translate or manifest as he matured. Would he become self-conscious and dampen down his true nature, or would it remain intact with some clever adjustments for times when he needed to rein it in?

As it transpires (and as I suspected), the formality and restraint of secondary school is a massive struggle for him. Not socially, of course not. It is the social interaction, the banter, the connections with older teens in particular, that make going to a large state school bearable. His gregarious nature is at home moving among different groups, and his sharp wit and humour are appreciated and welcomed.

The struggle is in conforming. Following the rules, staying quiet in class, wearing uniform correctly, and doing what he absolutely has no interest in. As he amasses behaviour points (negative) and detentions, and even internal exclusions, the frustration builds and he asks me if something is wrong with him.

I am churned up inside observing this. I feel that he's grossly misrepresenting himself and suffering for it.

I tell him that he has to learn to play the game. Smart and savvy though he is, he hasn't yet learned to be seen to be complying. The urge to chat, and sing and dance, and make outspoken comments, overtakes his better judgment sometimes. The free spirit wants to stay free.

I find myself acting as a go-between – a mediator between school and Louie. That mother energy that I felt from moment one is rising high these days as I find a way to stand with, and support, Louie, while telling him home truths about his lack of respect and care for others. I'm full of fierce yet tender love for that sweet soul who is also a self-interested teenager who I, sometimes, momentarily don't like.

The independent one needs me to both let him go, but also to be right there. To fight his corner, yet be unbiased. I feel like I am being called upon to step right up to the plate, to show all I have got as a mother, so he never doubts my love for him; even as my passion to raise a decent human turns to exasperation with the tediously repetitive foibles, and occasional more serious incidents when I lose it. Often spectacularly.

This boy of mine highlights my shortcomings, pushes my triggers and reveals my own darkness; and at the same time, he's showing me where I can grow. I know that. Somehow, in the mess, I manage to find the words, the expression that is fitting to his emotional development and intelligence; and he grasps the depths of what I'm saying and it makes an impact. I am grateful for that. Grateful that we can talk on this level, and he hasn't become monosyllabic and detached from me.

This is exhausting yet gratifying. I remind myself that growing up can be hellish, with teenage hormones running amok creating chaos, and confusion in the mind and body that is changing at a rate of knots. All this, and a beautiful madcap jester who is taking time to master the art of still being himself, while attempting to adhere to the restrictions and conventionality within the quagmire of a vast, mainstream school. If it proves to be impossible, then he can leave; but just for now, we're taking the challenge. Together.

Even as I wonder who this lanky youth is that I share my home with and that replaced my little boy, I still give thanks every day. I like being around this guy, I like knowing him and I'm so privileged to be the one that is having the experience of being his mum. He makes me laugh hysterically and smile broadly. His current antics and questionable behaviour bring a nervous nausea, and sometimes the hot tears of frustration and upset fall uncontrollably.

But the love! Oh, the love. That's when I remember he's the same one. Despite the outward change, the deep voice, the surprising insecurity, and the need for privacy and space to explore without me, it's the unseen gossamer thread between us, containing the strength of power of the universe that arrived with that baby, that remains constant.

Unconditional love.

It can withstand anything.

Lesley Hughes

Second-time motherhood

I look at my second son sleeping peacefully, and experience a great sense of calm. I don't feel lonely, panicky, isolated – all the sensations that were so strong after my first child was born. I don't feel I'm pretending to be a mother. I just am a mother.

My desire for a second child was incredibly strong, probably exacerbated by being an only child, and the overwhelming sense when I was growing up that something was missing. In fact, the emotions that engulfed me when I became a mother were like re-opened wounds from my childhood. I was fearful that I would feel distanced from my second baby, mired in anxiety and uncertain at every turn.

I remember the sensation of being marooned in a big tunnel straight after the first birth, cocooned from reality by the effects of the epidural. I looked dispassionately at my partner and cousin as they exclaimed in emotional delight over the newcomer. I wanted to get cleaned up, to eat, to sleep. The midwife said, ''Let's get Mum up to the ward' and I thought, 'My Mum's not here, is she?' I couldn't get my head round the fact that I was 'Mum'. In the fog of the first few weeks, I kept thinking how hard everything was – I was conscious of being at odds with myself, although I'd give the impression that everything was fine. How on earth would I ever be able to manage two when I couldn't manage one? And yet, I desperately didn't want him to be an 'only'.

The birth was so quick second time that I had no time for drugs. This meant I had a triumphant rush of 'super-being-ness' straight after, that had been described to me by the only two mothers I knew who'd had drug-free births. I felt alive, vital, strong. After the event, I was too excited to sleep. I just kept looking at him with a rush of pure love. Now the rest of our lives could begin. The wounds of the first time seemed to have healed themselves.

I'd focused on my feelings for my newborn so much, I hadn't really considered how the relationship I'd have with my first child would change. We'd all talked about how to prepare him to cope with his new brother, but hadn't considered how we adults would react to the different dynamic. My partner's primary focus is still the elder, who can express his needs in words rather than wails. This was brought home to me recently when I went out one evening and stayed out a bit longer than I'd expected. I had a panicky phone call from him, saying the baby was crying and he didn't know what to do. I realised how much I'd learnt. You just do this! Or that! It's obvious. And yet it wasn't to him, even though we'd been through it once before.

With my first child, I was eager for the markers of development that proved he was 'normal' – first smile, sitting, crawling, feeding himself and so on. Feeling like a dinghy on a stormy sea, I looked for the anchors of these progressions to prove that I was doing it right. Was it obvious that I was finding it so difficult? That I watched other mothers who seemed so natural and close with their babies, while I was so unsure? Perhaps I was longing to get on to the part that was easier, that made sense, where my baby and I could connect. Eventually, the connections did come, as I expect they do for most new mothers, and I couldn't imagine my life without him; although it was a gradual stealing up on me, rather than a blinding flash.

Second time around, I was reluctant to see the signs that took him away from babyhood. Stronger than that – a sentimental part of me wishes he could stay a baby forever. The day I accepted he was too big for his Moses basket

Photo: Kerry Ghais

and would be better off in a cot, I was maudlin all afternoon. I had him packed off to college already in my mind. Perhaps he sensed this himself and woke more often in the night for the subsequent weeks, meaning I'd usually end up tucking him in next to me in order to gain precious sleep before the elder woke. To hell with the expert books that I'd been so hidebound by the first time that implied if you let the baby sleep with you, he'd never sleep alone, that is if he'd survived being squashed by you in the first place. He'd snuggle down next to me, with a look of pure contentment on his face. It seemed so natural, so right.

Breastfeeding the second time was so much easier, and I had a real sense of achievement that I managed to get to six months on my milk alone. He truly was what I made him. It was quite often hard to keep doing it, especially in the evenings when my three-year-old was tired after nursery and clamouring for my attention. I would get irritated when he stuck his head between mine and the baby, blocking my view of him. How could I get cross at my young child, who had

had all of my attention until now, and quite reasonably couldn't understand why this new impostor had muscled in? And yet, was I being too hard on myself? If anybody else had stuck their head in, I would have been quite justified in my snapping. Even your nearest-and-dearest have to accept the boundaries of personal space. But for the first months, you have to hold your baby close because they can't manage on their own. Their personal space is the same as yours because in some way they are still part of you. After that begins the gradual, and sometimes painful, sequence of letting go at various significant points of nursery or school.

The guilt still chimes in my head. I wonder if I am unable to share my love equally because, as an only child, I didn't experience the division of attention between me and a sibling. The assumption is often made that only children are spoilt, getting whatever they want, but the battle to get attention can often be greater, because you have to enter a different arena. An 'only' has to move in the realm of the adults, talk their language, adopt their customs, rather than the more understandable world of another child.

Is this how sibling rivalry starts? The little chippings-away at a mother's good humour? Your lack of patience because you are so, so tired after the baby's restless night of teething, then rudely awakened in the early morning by your older child who's had several hours of uninterrupted sleep? And yet again, how lucky you are to have two beautiful, healthy, wonderful children – how dare you complain, even for a second, because at any moment it might all be taken from you? So my mind goes on, like a mouse on its wheel, turning these thoughts over.

Is the ease with the baby due to being more relaxed, more settled in my role as a mother? He is not the complicated machine that has to be fed, changed and entertained correctly otherwise he will break down. With my first, I couldn't see the person behind all the tasks that had to be done, and yet, I was learning 'on the job' and did the best I could at the time. It is so easy for a mother to feel guilty, that she is doing everything wrong. I, like countless others, reached for manuals to reassure me, rather than trusting my instincts. Second time around, I feel more confident, I can read his 'signals', although I was always baffled as to what this meant before. It sometimes feels awkward if someone else is present and I have to articulate what I think is needed at a particular point. It's like learning to drive a car, or play the piano or type – if you look to see what your hands are doing or attempt to explain it to a bystander, you have trouble continuing.

I try to hide from the inevitable that this darling baby will, all too soon, be a truculent toddler, answering back, refusing to eat his greens, causing scenes in the supermarket – all the things that had made you tut before you became a parent yourself and knew the relentlessness of daily life. As I write, the baby is less than a year and is adorable, but he will soon be a 'terrible two'. Does nature programme a mother to be wrapped up in her defenceless new baby, to the exclusion of her other child(ren), for its own safety? Maybe the mixture of feelings I have now are as normal and natural as the overwhelming 'all-at-sea-ness' after the first birth…

When I was pregnant the second time, I spent the afternoon with a family who had a two-year-old and a baby. I'd known them when the first child came along and observed their delight over her, but not seen them recently, and was surprised to see that they were very sharp with the older child over what seemed to be small matters. The baby had all of the attention and the child seemed to be sidelined. I thought I wouldn't behave like that, but, like so many humbling experiences of becoming a mother, I find myself behaving exactly like that. I have to remind myself he is still very young and I am tired – the two together sometimes produce fireworks.

My elder is very protective and proud of his little brother, and the baby, in turn, lights up when he sees him. He accepts that he is not allowed to pick him up unless I'm there, and his concern when the baby is crying is almost as great as mine. Unconsciously, he adopts my language when calming him, 'It's alright, baby…,' or he will scuttle to fetch a favourite toy, or a dummy. Sometimes, he will grab one of the baby toys, insisting that it is his, which is, I imagine, a call for attention. At the moment, he is unquestionably 'top dog' in terms of skills and strength. I am slightly anxious about how he will respond when the baby is able to go for the toys himself and challenges the elder's authority. Hopefully the bond between them will be strong enough to overcome the spats.

Some of the sweetest moments are when I see him nestling up to the baby, whispering something to him or showing him a picture in a book. It is tinged with sadness, for there is a realisation that they will have a special bond as brothers that will exclude me in years to come. I'm thankful that they will have each other to confide in, and fervently hope that their relationship develops with the passing years and doesn't go sour. I am bursting with pride over my two boys; I will do my best to treat them both fairly and equally, and have faith that life will do so, too.

Maggie Gordon-Walker

16. How we can help

What does Mothers Uncovered do for women?

We get positive feedback every day; but what means the most to us is when women find help from each other via our network that sees them through the massive life change that is having children. Some, like Nicky, feel that they were brought back from the brink of postnatal depression. Others explain that they have found an outlet for self-expression. Claire Robinson says: 'Viewing motherhood through that lens encouraged me to give voice to my struggle, and to support other women, focusing them, valuing their work and acknowledging their fears, challenges and confusion.'

To be a mother
is to discover another in places there are no
spaces,
at least none to call mine.

It's to be constantly amazed
through the haze of exhaustion
at each new day's revelation and blooming.

To meet changes and challenges
and last-minute outfits
with smiles through tears of longing
for one whole sleep cycle,
clean dishes or a soak in a clean bath.

It's to notice how well you've turned out,
let go or not,
but feel for another
more than you ever knew you could.

To know you feel different,
accept it and not judge.
To strive for perfection,
let go of expectation –
our ruin and damnation.
To cry for our sins
and feel guilt for the least of things.

To stifle a sneeze, a scream, a shout,
not letting those words out.
To fall asleep smiling,
wake to crying,
drawing her close
and always, but always, finding ways to cope.

To survive a series of mini deaths,
salted cheeks smiling on memories
mourning that from which she's moved on,
greeting the next phase,
promising to always remember
never to forget what's already been.

To lay awake wide-eyed with worry
as a hot baby lays upon you
while you search and think maybe,
maybe I did or could have done something
wrong,
maybe this one won't be here for long.

To feel responsibility so strong, so depended
upon,
it spears you through your core,
sends you a fear-quake,
a tremor through your physicality,
an ache that make you feel so alone, so sore.

To find oneself alone amongst old friends,
a welcome worn out,
an alien, outsider in this new and foreign land,
though it looks just like home.
Something has happened,
something has changed.
An arrival.
It's me – a mother uncovered.
Hanora Power-Dow

I had reservations about coming, but I'm glad I did. It's very interactive and I wasn't sure how I'd be – I thought I might dip in and out of it. It's very real and very human. Everyone's story is so different, and it's empowering. I almost wish I'd been here before I gave birth so I'd realise anything could happen. No two stories are the same, and there's no perfect pregnancy, labour and birth and beyond.
Laura

I found a group at a time when I needed to express my feelings about motherhood. I didn't have the security within my own relationships to truly express my emotions and feelings about motherhood, without feeling like I was being judged. This group has taught me that many mums have exactly the same fears and anxieties, and that sometimes it's ok to feel this way. I feel not so alone any more and more content with my life. A truly valuable experience which pulled me from the brink of postnatal depression.
Nicky Walter

On 18 July 2014, our youngest daughter, Romy, died at the age of four months. There was no warning: no illness, no symptoms, no doctor's visit. My pregnancy had been of the usual gestation, the birth was beautiful and she was a happy, healthy baby girl. On the morning of 17 July, she and I visited a local café where we had a lovely time. By lunchtime, she was unconscious and having a seizure; and by 4.15pm the following day, following hour after agonising hour of tests, waiting, and hoping, we had allowed her life support system to be switched off. She had

experienced a brain haemorrhage, and it was too sudden and too powerful for anything to reverse. For the ensuing two years, I was swallowed whole by a dense fog of grief, anger and unbearable pain.

During the time that I fell apart, I tried every type of counselling and therapy I could, just to save me from going under and to keep some vague kind of normalcy for our two older children. It was only when, early this year, I found myself at a writing group run by the wonderful Mothers Uncovered, that I began to understand that writing was the way forward for me. I started my blog, 'Remembering Romy', to help me to sift through my feelings; and, as my grief began to evolve, I became determined to use my experience, my blog and any other skills I could muster, to help others who find themselves members of this club that nobody wants to join.
Ali Norrell

I jumped at the chance to come to Mothers Uncovered – I didn't even think about it – I just knew I had to do it. There was a feeling that shocked me once, a feeling, a dread panic, of just, 'I've got to get out of here.' I would be amazed if there wasn't a mother alive, a parent alive, who didn't feel like that at some point.
Felicity Beckett

I would recommend the project to any new mum. It's learning, therapy, bonding and friendship, all in one. It provides an invaluable forum to swap experiences in a comfortable, open and non-judgmental environment. It puts your mind at rest and confirms your faith in your own ability as a mother. Motherhood should be celebrated, especially in modern society where it's been downgraded, and even demonised, by the media and government. This project offers a really positive and useful way to do that. The sense of self-worth the sessions provide is priceless, and I can see from the way the mothers blossomed by the end of the fourth session that it is something that will have an enduring impact. Mothers

Uncovered does more for the psychological wellbeing of mums than the health profession does throughout pregnancy and beyond.
Anonymous

An experience that unites mothers, strengthens bonds with their babies and families, and starts mini-revolutions.
Jo

Loss adjustment

Nearly three years into this mothering lark, and still the title 'mother' doesn't sit comfortably with me. It certainly doesn't come first in my mind as a self-descriptor, despite the praxis of mothering occupying the majority of my time. I feel strangely distanced from it, although I am approaching it. It evokes to me a passive, unnamed subject devoid of individuality or personality, one befitting a tabloid piece perhaps: 'Mother dies in headlong crash', 'Mother of two, 38, wins Nobel Prize'.

'Mother' is rarely a self-definition or deeply felt identity, but one that is imposed, denoting an identity fashioned from the needs and expectations of others. My sense of self following the seismic changes that becoming (and continuing as) a mother has wrought is more aptly described as 'woman struggling with small people and the changed expectations upon her', or 'woman surveying things with disbelief and panic, looking for mum and realising she is it'. The notion of a mother can be seen very differently, of course. As a verb, the word itself speaks of something active and vital, which is probably more like it. Moreover, the role of 'mother', with its various archetypes or caricatures, is embraced gratefully by many. It is a peculiar term, in that it means so much (as it signals the power and commonality of the female reproductive experience, biologically and socio-culturally), but in itself tells so little about the person behind it.

Last year, I returned to a small Brighton room and met a group of women – the room felt less cramped than two years before when there had been half the number there. My

baby, who I had clutched and shushed throughout the sessions with the first group, was now starting to seem a girl, and not there. Another child was residing in my belly and threatening to descend into my life any day. All those I met had two or more children, all 'wise-end' examples of the way forward for me. We shared the concerns of our days and weeks, and were led in mindfulness practice in a sanctuary of sorts. It helped usher me into my second round of motherhood wonderfully.

The first time I had entered that space, the profile of the women I met was equally fortuitous; we were all first-timers with children born within a two-week period. Both facilitators had just one child, but were much further on in their journeys. We were all at around 12 weeks post-birth, reeling with the eruption of the newborns we rocked and the weight of expectations. We all felt our relationships with ourselves, partners and families had changed forever, and needed to explore that loss and adjustment; we also craved a space to revisit our experiences of birth and the immediate postnatal period.

We found somewhere where we were capably guided, in a non-judgmental manner, to scratch at revealing the women we were before motherhood hit us, and to explore what was left and what we wished to recover or transform. We were able to reflect and reframe experience safely and unashamedly, using the conduit of writing. We were provided with references and examples of women who had gone before us and documented the terrain: creative women seeking to reclaim themselves and provide testimony from the front lines. For me, I found a space to speak relatively unfiltered, express anger and bewilderment, and feel at one in a room of women for possibly for the first time in my life.

Once I learned of Mothers Uncovered, I knew instantly that I must attend. I encountered Maggie's strongly worded petition around the time of my daughter's birth, then read her Guardian article and website, gleaning that a discussion and writing course was starting soon. This particularly appealed as I understand the world and my experiences best in relation to the written word. The whole process proved invaluable, with guided exercises and opportunities for exploration, facilitated by fantastic women, at a time when I would not have otherwise harnessed the emotion and confusion within me on to the page, or out of my mouth.

I had hitherto made it to a few local baby groups, with Rhymetime proving the most successful (being reasonably short, starting late and entirely structured, with no real expectation of sociability). It allowed me to survey the array of newish mothers thrown up within the local area and feel some sense of not being alone. Singing songs and shaking instruments does something positive for the soul, but I still came away feeling disturbed, short-changed by the lack of connection in the room.

During the first Mothers Uncovered session, we were supported to introduce ourselves and set our stalls out somewhat. I distinctly recall the unease I felt as I trimmed the corner from the formula carton I needed to quieten my daughter and tipped it into a bottle – shame rising as my fellow mothers were both capably feeding on their breasts. I felt liberated of my discomfort as I gave voice to that feeling – and hopefully contributed to their understanding. Over the coming weeks, we shared vignettes and visions of ourselves, and put down words on paper, despite the distractions of those that drooled and mewled. We spoke freely of our fears in relation to seemingly selfish concerns, of never following our art or dreams, or feeling ourselves again. We'd all been knocked sideways by motherhood and reaped the benefits of conducting a collective welfare check, where we could be respectfully heard over generous selections of refreshments. Our babies' needs and development remained secondary, but were an utterly necessary condition of it all. Gratefully, our connection continues to this day.

Having my second child, I still felt aftershocks from the first, but had the benefit of some plateauing behind me. I felt greater trust in my own judgment, in a position to use

the past to inform and future to direct me; but with the wisdom to appreciate the necessity of residing firmly in the present (linking nicely to the mindfulness focus of the group). Following edifying discussion and snacks, we undertook a short practice, allowing me a rare chance to commune with the baby inside me and the body housing her, away from the demands of work and a toddler.

With a history of mental health issues and a great many years feeling adamant that motherhood would not be for me, I think I knew it would entail a struggle. I understood the gravity of it, so I sought to avoid it, maintaining that I saw myself as an old woman in a room full of books. All changed when, predictably, I felt that mid-30s urge and slight panic.

Still, the entire enterprise (each time) was not wholly planned. Discovering my first pregnancy shocked the life out of me, literally; a week later, I experienced early miscarriage and was left reeling as I processed it all. That was my first personal encounter with the power of it all, I guess.

Having been a student midwife, and up close to the horror of pregnancy, baby loss, labour and postnatal mental ill-health, I had a realistic appreciation of how it all went. I'd taken keen interest in the Confidential Enquiry into Maternal Death reports collated with the charming Ronseal-esque title 'Why Mothers Die' (see also CEMACH, CMACE and MBRACE-UK). I'd learned that a leading cause of death for new mothers was suicide, and was unsurprised that the profile of those most likely affected was middle class, mid-30s and educated: the 'high expectations lot' – women sold the lie that their 20s must be for cocktails, careers and cohabitation, with children waiting until later. A significant number of women at high risk of mental ill-health are those with IVF, rainbow or otherwise much sought-after pregnancies. Being mid-30s working class, with a middle-class education and milieu, I knew to treat motherhood with the reverence it deserved.

I felt affronted by the way mental illness was framed within midwifery theory and practice.

Photo: Kerry Ghais

The medical profession respects a simplistic typology of baby blues, PND and puerperal psychosis, with antenatal depression creeping in deservedly for attention. The lack of understanding and insight shown by my peers, teachers, mentors and other professionals was stark, even though the notion of PND was brought up all the time.

Midwives and health visitors were very well-meaning, but disposed to see it as a discrete episode, resolvable via submission to a course of treatment that would return women to their old selves, a convenient label serving to subdue voices even further than the experience itself. I bore witness to how a woman with 'query puerperal psychosis' was treated, privy to the tacit contempt and bemusement at ward handover. I saw a highly anxious and distressed woman denied the means to process and express her experience. She was traumatised following a forceps delivery, ruptured cervix and subsequent surgery, and reluctant to see the son she

expressed milk for (which her devoted mother fed him), while petrified that her undercarriage was splitting open. I accompanied a midwife who refused the woman a pen and paper so she could record details about her care and track feeding.

I happily gave her mine and spent as much time as possible with her. The psychiatric team eventually conceded she wasn't psychotic, so the excitement at handover diminished. I recall the words 'highly strung' and 'pathetic' being used. As she left the ward with her family, I urged them all to look after each other and recognised her distress as a rational response to a life-changing event. Back then, though, I couldn't understand what she was headed home to: those first few weeks and months that blindside and bludgeon you. She would have benefited from a Mothers Uncovered group. Soon after that, I chose not to continue in midwifery.

Mothers Uncovered is testament to the way in which the creative process and expression is vital to health, and I mention the group to all new mums I know. Becoming a mother messes with you, no matter how thoroughly you research and plan, how relevant your emotional or practical experience, how much stuff you acquire, or how much support is on offer. Even the most realistic expectations will need revision; the clearest thinkers will acquire brains like balls of matted wool that need unravelling. In time, it is possible to fashion something nice out of them, with or without a pattern, but a knitting circle sure helps.

In fact, once the shit dies down, there is often an abundance of creativity, resourcefulness and enterprise attached to mothers, arising in different ways. There's the, 'If not now, when?' aspect to pursuing long-held hopes and dreams; the desire to harness the power and potential realised by producing people; the omnipresent inward pressure around role-modelling to your kids; and, of course, the economic imperatives that make flexible income gathering a necessity.

Attending Mothers Uncovered showed me the value of peer support and applying a critical approach to the mothering endeavour. It served as an invaluable induction into my new life, and instilled a confidence to develop and maintain relationships with a diverse network of women. Viewing motherhood through that lens encouraged me to give voice to my struggle, and to support other women, focusing them, valuing their work and acknowledging their fears, challenges and confusion.

I feel able to glimpse the woman behind every mother I encounter and not feel alienated, judgmental or competitive, no matter how they present or mask; to offer a kind word and speak with an honesty that names the elephant in the room. Simply saying, 'It's bloody hard isn't it?' or, 'Well done for getting here/keeping them alive' to women frantic in their exhaustion and efforts to convey ease, seems to engender such relief and connection, in ways that the sharing of baby milestones and weight-loss tips doesn't. My mind often returns to the faces and voices that I knew in that room; I think it always will.

Claire Robinson

Mothers Uncovered is a hugely essential growing supportive network of mothers, so that we can all together feel empowered and nurtured. This was something I have been yearning to see as I have been adjusting over the last two years to becoming a single mother to my 20-month-old.

As women, we can be emotional creatures. It would seem that we, more so than men, have an obvious need to express emotions that rise within us. By articulating or verbalising to another, we feel a huge release. The importance of this release during motherhood is huge, yet varies of course between individuals. If we don't articulate and process the deep emotions and feelings that childbirth, for example, can bring up, we might inadvertently hamper our own mental wellbeing, and perhaps inflict some of the negative build-up on our children. I say this with regret, of course – that it is the reality, from my own experience and my observations of other mothers, often lone parents with all the tremendous pressure of parenthood on their shoulders.

We battle with maintaining some sort of calm and patience throughout all the challenges we experience, while raising our children and dealing with other life pressures.

The opportunity for me to express some of what I have experienced as a single mother has been massive. To have the chance to do just that within the warm, relaxed and gentle environment that Mothers Uncovered has offered, has made the release ever more meaningful. It has, in effect, allowed me to process and to move on from negative states of mind, and to deal with some challenges with a more positive outlook.

Not only this, but by beginning my release, so to speak, I have, in fact, begun to write more songs, now on the subject of motherhood. I do so myself, to share, to express and to connect with other mothers who have experienced, or are experiencing, similar situations. By communicating, we can become a supportive entity for each other, and we can work to reduce or remove feelings of despair and isolation which can lead to depression.

Lou Noble

Isolation, support and hope

As Naomi Stadlen points out in her wonderfully supportive book, 'What Mothers Do', there has never been a time in history when mothers have faced more isolation. Many of us are geographically removed from our extended family, or unable to access support from them due to their own work and life commitments, or to strained family relationships. Among the 22 mothers I interviewed for my book, 'Wild Motherhood: Tending the Fire of your Creative Spirit', and the many mothers I've worked with in groups, loneliness, isolation and lack of support were frequent themes.

Like Merav, mother-of-three, who was thrown into isolation by the birth of her first baby. She experienced trauma at birth and had a 'very needy baby'.

'I was in isolation, and quite depressed. It wasn't hard looking after the baby, but the isolation was hard. I had to do it, that was my job.'

Merav's isolation was compounded by not having any women in her life. She had a difficult relationship with her mother, although she was supportive in a practical sense.

As mothers, particularly in the early months and years, we need each other more than ever; we need communities of mothers and women who support each other, and share our burdens. In the words of Gemma, another interviewee for my book: 'I miss the tribe! I feel we now are asked to live this motherhood in a very unnatural way, mostly being on our own and having to play all areas of life. In this process of individualisation and families living separate from each other, I know we lost a lot; and my cells miss the sharing of the roles and the group support, the wisdom of the elders, and the joy of more kids than mine around.'

But there are encouraging signs of mothers forming networks of support – not just online, because, as valuable as networks such as Mumsnet are, there's nothing like a hug, a coffee in someone's kitchen, and a friend who will come and cook for you when you're so exhausted you're in tears. Antenatal classes and mum-and-baby groups, while useful sources for connection, are usually more about birth and parenting skills than the experience of the mother. Unlike groups like Mothers Uncovered, the openness and honesty can be hard to come by. And if you want a space to share your feelings and experiences more deeply, unfortunately, there is often stigma attached to attending groups specifically for postnatal depression, when the reality is that many mothers experience depression.

I was inspired to hear that a woman who attended one of my writing and discussion groups for mothers had set up an informal group where mothers go over to each other's houses once a week to help with any household tasks. This lightened the sense of drudgery by adding companionship and fun – as well as sharing the care of the children. Practical and emotional support rolled into one.

But real support from other mothers isn't always easy to come by. If you want to reconnect with your work or creative pursuits, it becomes even more important to find space to offload the stresses and tensions of the eternal juggling, as well as share practical support through childcare swaps: mothers who can admit the difficulties of being a mother as well as the joys. 'It helps if you have a supportive partner, although my husband worked full time, so it was up to me to organise structures like childcare,' says Petra, a mother-of-three who mostly used au pairs to enable her to work in photography and other creative fields. Kat, another mother-of-three, couldn't have done it without the support of a great childminder, and Bela's husband gives support with childcare: 'I feel really lucky to have had his support – I know I need that support to be able to do it.'

But this terrain is far from simple. The idea of partners as supporters can also be riddled with disappointed expectations and resentments. As mothers, we often face the loss of financial and domestic equality that comes with our role in a society that values wage-earning over care-giving. In the words of Merav: 'Suddenly paths diverged with Sandy [her husband]. They had been equal up to that point.'

Rebecca Asher argues in her brilliant book, 'Shattered', that parenting, the 'work of love', demands compromise, and this is the price we pay for a 'richer life and a fulfilling relationship with our children'. But, she continues, 'It is women who pay this price much more than men, and who, therefore, lack the opportunity to develop their careers and personal interests to the same degree.' This is because, 'they take on the work of the private sphere in a way fathers do not', due to a combination of factors, such as social policies and economic pressures that continue to make it difficult for fathers to fully share parenting responsibilities. And even with the financial support to pay for childcare, for many mothers it simply feels too difficult to hand their young baby over to someone else when it is her, and only her, that her child is wanting.

Our relationships are always shifting, particularly in the early years of motherhood. Being a mother in a society where mothering isn't recognised, celebrated and supported the way it should be, means we often have to find and create the networks we need to sustain and hold ourselves. But this process can be a catalyst for creativity and new possibilities as we break out of our isolation and find that we aren't, after all, alone in our struggles with motherhood.

Morgan Nichols

Mindfulness and Mothers Uncovered

I'm stressed. You're stressed. Everyone is busy and stressed all the time, so mothers often feel they have no right to lay claim to being more stressed than anyone else. However, if you factor in the lack of sleep that most mothers, definitely new mothers, contend with, not to mention the responsibility for their families they feel is theirs to shoulder alone, plus the constant roll call in their heads as to what is needed for the next activity from the moment they wake up, it is understandable that contemplation of the here and now is a far cry from their oft frantic state.

At the mindfulness eight-week course I attended, we discovered the constant thinking ahead and back was not conducive to living in the here and now one iota. We needed time, a minimum of twenty minutes a day, to sit and just be. 'But when will I have time to sit and just be?' wails our poor beleaguered mother, even though she knows that, to function better, she must take time for herself.

It's not at all easy, which is why I developed a new five-week course for Mothers Uncovered to introduce some of the concepts of Mindfulness, and to allow mothers those precious few minutes to focus inwards.

The groups have to centre on the written aspects, rather than long meditations, as participants usually have babies with them who demand their attention. Yet we always manage to fit in five minutes to meditate, or sit quietly holding babies, which seems to calm the babies as much as their mothers.

We realise that a lot of time is taken up with comparisons and judgments, of ourselves and others. Have I managed better as a mother today? Have I managed to do lots of other things? Mindfulness isn't about trying to eliminate all the bad thoughts and feelings, but allowing what's in your head to be there. The trouble for mothers is, there is usually a judgment involved in their ruminations – 'I don't like what is happening' or 'Why can't I manage to do that?' They look around and see only other mothers who are coping much better, or so it seems. They feel they must be the most disorganised and it reflects badly on their parenting. If they were a truly good mother, so their exhausted brain goes, they would be able to do a hundred tasks every day on four hours' broken sleep.

Mothers find themselves with greater levels of dependence in their lives: their baby's dependence on them, their dependence on partners to support them, their own sudden lack of independence – too late they realise how joyous it was to just get up and go without a moment's thought. Participants come to realise the impact their thoughts have on their feelings. This is especially true of motherhood, when we are forever trying to keep up with changing circumstances and inevitably feel we're failing. If you can be aware of the thoughts as they come to you, you can see they are just events in your mind, rather than hard facts.

Photo: Kerry Ghais

Mothers often struggle with feeling hopeless – they will NEVER gain any autonomy back. The great deal of effort spent in trying to push away unwelcome experiences would be better spent accepting experiences as they happen, whether they are good or bad. The word 'acceptance' is problematic because it implies resignation to an undesirable state. However, acknowledging an experience or feeling doesn't mean the same as wanting or liking it, it is just recognising it is there. If we try to resist by thinking, 'I should be able to cope,' this reinforces negative thoughts about ourselves, rather than compassion. Instead of berating themselves when unwelcome thoughts crowd in, participants try and establish whether they are judging themselves, setting unachievable standards or expecting perfection.

It is paramount for mothers to take care of themselves in order to take care of others. Sometimes they can get overwhelmed by anxiety, stress and fear. Especially when they are always rushing from place to place and are constantly thinking about their child or children. When we are feeling overwhelmed, it can be helpful to tell ourselves that it will not stay that way. Life is uncertain, everything changes, there will be good times and bad times.

We collectively make a list at the end of the session of a small step they could take today to contribute to their wellbeing, plus a longer list of the things they need each day to be 'as well as possible.' When asked, 'How does that suggestion make you feel? What is your attitude to yourself right now?', it is gratifying to see them more at peace with themselves.
Maggie Gordon-Walker

Holding up the world

Claire Robinson

I could attempt to write here a wryly observed account of the personal change (and devastation) that ensued on becoming a mother. I won't, though, as I am both bewildered by the enormity of that challenge, and keenly aware that it has been done so comprehensively and exquisitely, with great pathos and humour, by many wonderful women. The blogosphere, social media commentators and authors of longer written studies have excised the belly of the matter. What I want to pick at here is the structural power relations we are subject to as mothers. I have been a feminist forever; a radical one, at that. I have Adrian Mole to thank, or rather his mum Pauline. It was reading Adrian's diary (penned by the marvellous Sue Townsend) that first raised my consciousness: I read with fascination about Pauline's late onset conversion to Women's Lib and dungarees, and her lovechild with a middle name of Germaine. A few years later, I sought out 'The Female Eunuch' at the local library (disgusted that my mum hadn't even heard of it) and got my hands on a Dworkin, and there was no looking back. It wasn't difficult to discern the roots of the oppression of the female sex class, growing up as a working class girl in Thatcher's Britain with two older brothers and a maladjusted father.

Capitalism is a product of patriarchy, and together they have situated us. The Marxist in me acknowledges that women have long been burdened with bearing the load of reproducing and maintaining of the family unit, assuring the next generations of workers and stabilising the male. Industrialisation created a need for isolated, geographically-mobile and self-sufficient nuclear families. Unsurprisingly, women, who undertake the not insignificant matter of growing and birthing children, have typically copped the lot in regards to nurturing said offspring. We can be thankful to our foremothers for hard-won social change and equalities – legislation that facilitates our freedom and social justice today. However, alongside that progression has been an interesting development of parenting (read 'mothering') as a subject of study. From Dr Spock via Gina Ford, Supernanny, the attachment crew and gentle folks, to a whole host of studies and articles, parenting has been thoroughly dissected and disseminated into 'philosophies' and 'approaches' for the consumer age. Efforts to support parents with scientific or evidence-based knowledge are, of course, noble and helpful; but these paragons of parenting have reflected diminished support networks. They speak to the anxious, paranoid and identity-seeking, where once the words and wisdom of elders might have garnered

These paragons of parenting have reflected diminished support networks more respect, and there might have been greater confidence and trust in one's intuition. The family (and mother role) has been subject to significant study, and there has, arguably, been a fetishisation of motherhood occurring alongside the faux liberation of women within labour markets. Social progress within the prevailing economic climate only achieved women the double burden of work and family, socialised as we are into habitually bearing the domestic mental load.

Continual challenge

Thus, we find ourselves at a time when virtual villages are assembled – gin-raising, hat-tipping and advice- (and selfie-) sharing spaces for mothers – vital networks of women to support and sustain their peers in the face of the continual challenge that is motherhood. The exemplar for these, Mumsnet, has been a truly political force (the Women's Institute bears mention, too, with its long tradition as an assembler and facilitator of activism). Forums and blogs contain a raw mixture of self-promotion, catharsis, support-seeking/giving, compassion, acceptance and identity/tribe-forming. Much of their output covers what often goes unsaid about mothering (the activity) and motherhood as an institution, and is at turns touching and hilarious; always relatable – affirmative and lifesaving words to many, I am sure.

Motherhood confronts you with so much hitherto avoided or unseen: yourself, the identity you have concocted, your position in the world, your mother or other significant women; and all other women, with whom you share important commonalities of experience in relation to biology and socialisation. This includes the likelihood of direct harm from the men of the world: violence against women and girls is rightly judged a human rights issue; and so-called domestic or intimate partner violence (including coercive control) often begins during a woman's pregnancy, increasing with subsequent ones. Women's reproductive rights are managed by men (in political suits and white coats); and pregnancy and birth are subject to such considerable medicalisation that

> Motherhood confronts you with so much hitherto avoided or unseen

can be argued to exert patriarchal control (and abuse) over women's bodies and experience.

Despite the ubiquity (and necessity) of mothers, they are often marginalised, rendered invisible or unheard; and having children of your own reveals this clearly in so many ways. It develops compassion and empathy in your relationship with the world, alongside heightened fears and risk aversion. It changes the way you interact and appear to others, affecting how you take up physical space and give voice, obfuscating or displacing the person you were before (or the one you appeared to be). It also changes the way women can, or do, organise and assemble. It is a very perverse position that women find themselves in: wanting or feeling the need to have children, and wanting to nurture them as a primary carer; but also being compelled to pursue and maintain careers (or, more specifically, wage earning), not only in attempt at self-esteem, self-sufficiency or self-actualisation, but by pure economic necessity. It is a cruel feature of modern parenting that so many families require two full time (or thereabouts) incomes to maintain mortgages and lifestyles, while armies of other women (including grandmothers, middle-aged mothers and young low-waged women) are paid, or not, to look after their children from babehood.

'What we do'

The midwife who supported me in labour with my first child told me, 'It's what we do'; and women have long known that and got on with it, which is to be celebrated. Naomi Stadlen documents the labour, commitment and heart-work of mothers in 'What Mothers Do and How Mothers Love', and goes some way to capturing the confusion and conflicting emotions concerned. In 'The Mask of Motherhood', Susan Maushart dispels any romanticised notions of modern motherhood, building upon the foundation of Adrienne Rich's influential study, 'Of Woman Born', which addresses 'the power and powerlessness embodied in motherhood in patriarchal culture'. See also the recent Purplestocking movement, spearheaded by Vanessa Olorenshaw with Liberating Motherhood.

These critical voices notwithstanding, I believe there is too much in the way of pretence, resignation and martyrdom from women in their daily lives, in relation to their shift into a mothering role. See the wealth of mothering blogs and social media forums, and the quiet desperation and faux-hilarity within them. These platforms do provide (in)valuable, seemingly non-judgemental and supportive communities to women; and are opportunities within women-only space for much needed back-slapping, compassion and making sense of fear, guilt and shame.

It is immensely sad that women can't even feel they can be frank with social and health care professionals; but then they can't often be frank with themselves

However, they rarely, if ever, provide space to reflect upon the structural inequalities, deep injustices and dissatisfactions at play; or to question the decision to have a child (or the role of society in constructing that decision). Instead, women are all too easily persuaded (by peers and professionals in equal measure) that they might have PND or PTSD/birth trauma and need medical support, should consider their partner's mental health (or sexual) needs more, should adopt an alternative parenting philosophy or approach, should spoil themselves somehow (usually by attending to their personal grooming), or should down some gin every night. There is all too often a performative, identity-seeking element, which is totally understandable once the role of mother is adopted; but saddening, all the same. Whilst it is imperative women feel supported to feel that #YouGotThisMama, it is disheartening to note that women as a class still accept injustice and repression on such a scale as is involved on their mothering paths.

Hoodwinking

I firmly believe that women need to be enabled to channel their confusion, anger and bitterness positively, and to be heard. Too often, women are labelled as mentally ill or morally bankrupt when they feel, or express, their honest responses to motherhood under patriarchy and the prevailing economic system. There is a lot of hoodwinking and betrayal in operation; and as girls and women are socialised to behave and seek approval (not to mention tend and nurture their young), so much goes unchallenged, particularly within everyday experiences and interactions. Women are also well-schooled in policing each other in that regard, whether they are aware of it or not, and such norms and values are culturally reproduced. Perhaps this is in part due to our foremothers understanding the painful consequences of addressing the status quo all too well? Not to mention too many of them being burned at the stake or withering in the workhouse. It is immensely sad that women can't even feel they can be frank with social and health care professionals; but then they can't often be frank with themselves.

Sadness, fear, anxiety, depression, anger – these are all quite rational responses to the massive change and loss involved with becoming a mother. Women need to feel free to express and process them without prejudice, derision, guilt or shame. Alongside evidence-based advice and practical supportive services, they deserve access to networks of peers and channels for self-advocacy, harnessing creativity and releasing potential. This should include rallying political will and lobbying for change to foster greater recognition of the mothering role; and permit families to determine how they wish to organise parenting in the early years, and not be prevented by economics.

It is obscene that a culture and social structure has evolved where breastfeeding is taboo or marginalised: where women need their consciousness raised, and practical advice and support groups, to undertake this basic mammalian function. It is also outrageous that formula feeding has been mis-sold in so many ways (as an ideal or panacea, a liberator or enabler, or an evil). I say this as a mother with experience of both.

The best options

I find it concerning that the apparently enlightened among us have tendencies towards espousing prescriptive approaches that may appear innovative, authentic or liberating, but can prove oppressive. Whilst 'extended' breastfeeding, baby-wearing, co-sleeping, attachment philosophies (as distinct from 'attachment theory' proper), and elimination communication etc., may all provide admirable and effective methods, they aren't always the best option for all women, across all circumstances, and can prove limiting. However, a certain section of the population seems to be exerting a pressure on themselves to apply them, and persevere against any challenges to them, to their own detriment at times, often veering towards zealotry in their advocacy of them. Although this can promote important sisterhood and activism to some degree, paradoxically, it can practically amount to the control and restraint of women's power.

Women often lack the confidence to follow their intuition, and utilise strategies and techniques familiar and comfortable to them

Some of these methods may be extremely difficult to achieve under present times (with the lifestyles, expectations and punishments of our socio-economic system); and women can be seen exhausting themselves (and alienating themselves from each other and others) to undertake practices that fit idealised circumstances, or berating themselves for not applying them – all this in the first couple of months and early years of the shit-show that is motherhood, with scant appreciation of the marathon parenting actually entails.

It is sad that women often lack the confidence to follow their intuition, and utilise strategies and techniques familiar and comfortable to them, or in keeping with their personal and family histories, regardless of what the books say, or their friend is doing. Instead, many new mothers bandy about concepts and abbreviations, and exhibit a rigid appreciation of them, fearful of judgment or derision, attempting to prove something that is not under examination – their commitment and devotion to their children's needs.

As women progress as mothers, very few are able to stop to reflect and uncover themselves, let alone declare themselves and their trials, or organise and act collectively to bring about change for those who follow after. Those that attempt to, deserve to be heard as the truth-tellers they are.

The Mothers Uncovered journey

Maggie Gordon-Walker

How did Mothers Uncovered start?

It is the result of a process that started when I became a mother in 2004. Like many women, I had focused solely on the birth of my child, not seeing that my life would be changed forever from that point. After my second child was born in 2008, I set up a creative support network for (mostly new) mothers as a project for Livestock, a charity that I co-founded (www.livestock.org.uk). I thought it essential to have a group for mums that wasn't entirely focused on the baby/child. Of course Mothers Uncovered participants talked about their offspring - but in the context of the whole person - because behind every mother is the woman she has always been.

It was only intended to run for three groups in that year, but I subsequently met many women who wanted to attend and so it continued. It has grown to include several other past participants as facilitators. We have helped hundreds of women with our events and creative peer support groups focused on the mother, rather than the baby. Contrary to the beliefs that some might hold, the groups comprise a range of ages, personal circumstances and social and cultural backgrounds.

Aren't there lots of mother and baby groups?

There are, but these are often informal drop-ins, not suitable for addressing issues that might be difficult or painful. Discussion usually centres around the children, and mothers often report the impression that everyone is coping except them. There are also postnatal depression groups, but these carry a stigma of 'not coping'; and a fear that someone is keeping tabs on you because you are usually referred by a doctor or health visitor. There is a big hole between these two extremes, and we do our best to stem that gap, believing that most new mothers in fact have 'new motherhood syndrome', in which it's completely normal to be blissfully happy one minute and in the depths of despair the next. When a woman gives birth, the focus shifts to the baby. Women may be delighted and grateful to be mothers, but they need an outlet for the emotions generated by the enormous event they have experienced.

What's the idea behind Mothers Uncovered?

Firstly, it's to provide a support service to mothers through workshops and arts projects. We give women the chance to talk openly and honestly about their feelings and experiences, without fear of judgment.

Secondly, we want to give women the chance to celebrate and mark this point in their lives. It is very easy for a new mother to feel sidelined by the focus that is naturally placed on the baby, and to have difficulty expressing her feelings in a way that can also be creative.

Participants attend a series of structured sessions to facilitate more in-depth conversation. Some of our groups are for first-time mothers, but they are mostly aimed at women at any and all stages of motherhood. Sometimes, women don't feel the need to process their experiences until much later. This is often shared with others through exhibitions and performances. This helps

Photo: Kerry Ghais

to build self-esteem and to validate a woman's perspective. It also brings the often hidden nature of motherhood into the open.

Who runs the sessions?

Each group has two facilitators. They are all past participants of Mothers Uncovered. We are not affiliated to the NHS or any other bodies, so do not have access to any information about participants unless they choose to provide it. The facilitators are not 'perfect' mothers. Such a thing does not exist. They are going through the motherhood journey too, but are just a bit further along. Nor are the sessions telling participants how to be a mother. There is a wealth of information out there telling you that. We offer peer support. Hopefully, some lasting friendships will be made within the group; but, at the very least, participants will have had the opportunity to express the thoughts they might not be able to share with others in their lives.

What happens in the sessions?

The group is informally run, sitting on comfy chairs (if possible!). Each person shares something from their week. Further discussion takes place in pairs and within the group on specific topics, such as body image, relationships with others or how mothers are presented in the media. Depending on which course it is, there will be further writing, art, singing, mindfulness or drama exercises. There is the opportunity to share birth stories, if desired.

Are the sessions a drop-in?

No. We believe it's important to build up a sense of community and safety within the group, which can only be done if participants know the others that will be coming along. Women meet weekly for five weeks in the same group. It helps hugely that those who are running the groups are not present as experts or providing advice.

Participants quickly feel able to open up as they realise they are not the only ones struggling - they begin to feel less isolated, and start to take ownership of their lives and decisions. In the words of a past participant, 'Mothers Uncovered fills a gap you didn't even know was there.'

How is Mothers Uncovered funded?

Our parent company, Livestock, is a charity so we apply for grants. However, the funding is quite precarious and we have had to introduce charges for our courses in order to continue, but we keep them as low as we can. Course fees help to cover some of the costs of the venue, refreshments and materials, facilitators and publicity. There are always two free places per course and the concession rate is quite generous.

If you'd like to make a donation, we'd be very grateful. You can donate via Paypal to admin@livestock.org.uk or via Localgiving.

Why is Mothers Uncovered needed?

I set up a petition on Change.org three years back, which sits there quietly gathering a signature every now and then. It details how 'when the mother's needs are not met, nor are those of her family. PND has been associated with an increase in family conflict and has a detrimental impact on a partner's mental health, as well as causing financial problems. The impacts of perinatal mental health problems on children include emotional difficulties and behavioural problems, and special educational needs. You may think if you're not a parent, this doesn't affect you. It does. You might not be a mother, but we all have, or have had, a mother, and your upbringing may affect you more than you realise.'

However, the only thing that might make anyone pay attention to the petition is the cost implication. According to the Maternal Mental Health Alliance's report in October 2014, inadequate maternal care costs the UK £8bn a year, with a comparatively modest £337m required to tackle it. Why, I ask, are we playing catch-up instead of investing in preventative measures?

Every mother makes different choices. Not all of us want the same birth experience, for example. It is, however, wholly depressing how many women I meet who end up with emergency Caesareans when they'd desired a home birth. And woe betide them if they feel the need to talk about the trauma they've been through for some months afterwards. And, also could they please not breastfeed anywhere in public, travel on any public transport with their mewling infant and stop leeching the public purse with their endless demands...

Anyway, Rome wasn't built in a day: we do what we can. And what I can do is provide a space for mothers to talk about their experiences with their peers, making friendships and feeling less alone. We sometimes ask participants to name mothers in the public eye who might be considered role models. There is always a thoughtful silence as they cast their mind over the various actresses, presenters, singers etc and concede that none of these women are shown mothering (although perhaps Jacinda Ardern, New Zealand's pregnant prime minister, might change that). In general, though, even when they are in their 43-page 'Hello!' feature special, everything is perfect, everything is manufactured. This maybe wouldn't matter, if it weren't for the fact that the 99% of mothers who are not in the public eye feel inadequate next to these airbrushed lovelies. They feel fat, messy, exhausted, irritable, emotional. They ache all over. They wonder if they'll ever be anything beyond 'mum' again.

Mothers have a voice. Not the same one. There are millions of us, after all.

#letmumspeak